Kagaz & Kabza

AF379202

Sanjjay Jain

Printed in India

IndiePress

ISBN: 978-93-5776-955-6

First Printing, 2024

Indie Press

A division of Nasadiya Technologies Private Ltd.

Koramangala, Bengaluru

Karnataka-560029

http://indiepress.in/

Edited by Anagha Somanakoppa

Typeset by MAP Systems, Bengaluru

Book Cover designed by Vani Chandra

Publishing Consultant: Samyuktha Prasanan

Contents

Chapter 5: Strategic Mastery & Comprehensive Real Estate Navigator 183

ॐ

I humbly dedicate this book to almighty Shri Bhomiaji, Parasnath (Jharkhand) whose guiding omni presence to protect the land and blessings have illuminated our path throughout this journey. May this book serve as a beacon of knowledge and inspiration for all those who seek to navigate the complex landscape of real estate in India.

Disclaimer

General Information Purpose Only: The information provided in 'Kagaz & Kabza' by Sanjjay Jain is intended for general informational and educational purposes only. It is not designed to provide specific legal, tax, financial or any other professional advice.

No Professional Relationship: The content of this book does not constitute a professional relationship between the reader and the author or publisher. Readers should not act upon this information without seeking professional counsel from a licensed practitioner in their jurisdiction.

Limitation of Liability: The author and publisher disclaim any liability for any direct, indirect, incidental or consequential damages or losses that result from using or the inability to use the information in this book or the performance of the products recommended herein. This includes damages resulting from the application of the information on real estate decisions.

Accuracy and Completeness: While every effort has been made to ensure that the content of this book is accurate and provides valuable information, the author and publisher do not guarantee the accuracy of the content and are not responsible for any errors, omissions or inaccuracies. Information may become outdated as laws and practices evolve.

Use of Real Names and Third-Party Information:

- The book may include the real names of builders and other entities to provide authenticity and context as per publicly available reports and sources. These mentions are based on information obtained from reputable agencies and are not intended to defame or misrepresent any person or company.

- Inclusion of such names is for informational purposes only and does not imply any affiliation or endorsement by the individuals or companies mentioned.

- Prior consent from these entities for using their names has not been specifically obtained. If any entity or individual has concerns or objections regarding their inclusion, they are encouraged to contact the publisher for resolution.

Sources and Contributions: We acknowledge the contributions of various research firms operating in India to the field of real estate. While efforts have been made to include comprehensive and current information, inadvertent omissions of certain sources may occur. Readers are encouraged to consult additional sources to supplement the information provided.

No Endorsements: Reference to any specific commercial products, processes or services by trade name, trademark, manufacturer or otherwise, does not constitute or imply its endorsement, recommendation or favouring by the author or the publisher.

Acknowledgement of Terms: By using this book, readers acknowledge that they have read and understood this disclaimer and agree to its terms. Readers assume full responsibility for any actions taken based on the information provided herein and agree to use this book and its content at their own risk.

Acknowledgement

Writing a comprehensive real estate book requires the collaborative effort of many individuals, each contributing their expertise, insights and dedication. I extend my heartfelt gratitude to all those who played a significant role in the creation of this book, 'Kagaz & Kabza'.

First and foremost, I would like to express my deepest appreciation to my dear friend Rishabh Sawansukha for inspiring me to write this book and to Dr Anshul Dhingra for his invaluable guidance, mentorship and unwavering support at every step of this journey. Their wealth of knowledge and experience have been instrumental in shaping the content and direction of this book.

I would also like to extend deep gratitude to my dear son Divyansh Jain for his tireless efforts, insightful contributions and meticulous attention to detail.

I extend my deepest gratitude to my parents and my wife, Nity Jain, whose unwavering support and encouragement have been the guiding light on my journey of writing Kagaz & Kabza. Their love and affection have been my greatest source of strength and inspiration.

I owe a debt of gratitude to Shri. Motilal Oswal Ji, Managing Director & CEO of Motilal Oswal Financial Services Ltd. (MOFSL) and Shri. Vinod Dugar Ji, Co-promoter of the RDB Group, for their encouragement and wishes to go ahead with the concept of this book.

Further thanks go to the entire team who worked diligently behind the scenes to bring this book to life. From research and content creation to editing, design and publication, their collective efforts have resulted in a book that we are immensely proud of.

Lastly, to everyone who contributed, supported and believed in this project, I extend my heartfelt thanks. Your contributions have made 'Kagaz & Kabza' a reality.

With gratitude,
Sanjjay Jain

Foreword

In the dynamically evolving landscape of Indian real estate, where traditional values meet modern challenges, Sanjjay Jain's 'Kagaz & Kabza' emerges as a key publication that illuminates the path for navigating this complex sector. This book not only explores the architectural and economic transformations that have shaped Indian real estate but also arm its readers with the tools they need to succeed in today's market.

At its core, 'Kagaz & Kabza' is a profound narrative that intertwines India's rich real estate history with actionable strategies for the contemporary investor, homeowner and real estate professional. Sanjjay Jain, with his deep industry knowledge and expertise, addresses the various aspects of real estate dealings—from the intricate documentation required to secure one's investment to the strategic acumen necessary to capitalise on market opportunities.

The timing of Jain's manuscript could not be more opportune. As India stands on the brink of becoming a global economic powerhouse, its real estate sector presents unique opportunities and challenges. 'Kagaz & Kabza' serves as a bridge between the past and the future, offering a detailed examination of how historical practices influence current trends and how modern innovations are shaping the future of real estate in India.

The book is structured to cater to a wide range of stakeholders. For the novice homebuyer, it demystifies complex legal jargon and processes, making the daunting task of purchasing property more accessible and understandable. Seasoned investors will find value in the strategic insights into market trends and investment opportunities, backed by thorough research and analysis. Real estate professionals can deepen their understanding of the sector's regulatory environment, enhancing their ability to advise clients and manage transactions more effectively.

Sanjjay Jain introduces two pivotal frameworks in this book: 'KAGAZ' and 'KABZA'. These are not merely acronyms but are robust methodologies designed to ensure that every aspect of real estate ownership—from documentation to the assertion of property rights—is handled with utmost precision and care. 'KAGAZ' (Knowledge, Authentication, Guardianship, Accuracy and Zeal for updates) provides a comprehensive guide to property documentation. 'KABZA' (Knowledge, Agreements, Boundaries, Zero Discrepancies, Assurance) focuses on safeguarding property rights, ensuring that owners and investors can protect their assets effectively.

As you journey through the pages of 'Kagaz & Kabza', you will be equipped not only with the knowledge to navigate the complexities of property transactions but also with the confidence to make informed decisions. This book encourages a proactive approach to real estate dealings, emphasising foresight, preparedness and strategic planning.

I invite you to explore into 'Kagaz & Kabza' as more than a book—it is a strategic guide, a historical account and a visionary outlook for everyone who is part of or interested in the Indian real estate market. Let this book be your companion as you explore the exciting opportunities that real estate offers in one of the world's most vibrant economies.

Best Wishes

Vinod Dugar

Co-promoter, RDB Group

Foreword from the Editor

It is with great pleasure and anticipation that I introduce 'Kagaz & Kabza' by Sanjjay Jain, a captivating exploration into the complexities of real estate investment and management. Sanjjay Jain is a towering figure in the global real estate arena, known for his strategic foresight and entrepreneurial prowess that have significantly shaped global urban development.

In these pages, Sanjjay Jain shares his profound insights and expertise, honed over years of dedication to the field. From his strategic foresight to his entrepreneurial prowess, Sanjjay's approach to real estate innovation has left an indelible mark on the global urban development landscape. Drawing from his academic background and entrepreneurial ventures, Sanjjay masterfully blends technical expertise with entrepreneurial zeal, setting new benchmarks and reshaping industry standards along the way.

Sanjjay Jain's book doesn't just offer surface-level advice; rather, it explores deep into the intricacies of real estate investment and management, providing readers with a holistic 360-degree view of the field. Whether you're a seasoned investor or a newcomer to the industry, there is something in these pages for everyone.

What makes 'Kagaz & Kabza' truly invaluable is its relevance and timeliness. In an era marked by rapid urbanisation and shifting market dynamics, the need for expert guidance in real estate has never been greater. Sanjjay's astute observations and actionable advice provide readers with the tools they need to thrive in this dynamic environment.

Moreover, this book stands out for its holistic approach to real estate. Sanjjay goes beyond mere financial considerations to explore the social, environmental and ethical dimensions of property ownership and development. By emphasising the importance of sustainability, community engagement and ethical business practices, Sanjjay challenges readers to rethink their approach to real estate and consider the broader implications of their actions.

'Kagaz & Kabza' is more than just a guidebook; it's a manifesto for a new era of responsible and innovative real estate practices. This book will inspire all readers, irrespective of their background, to think differently about real estate and empower them to make informed decisions.

Warm regards,
Anagha Somanakoppa
Editor, Indie Press

Testimonials

"In 'Kagaz and Kabza', Sanjjay Jain embarks on a scholarly voyage, meticulously charting the evolution of Indian real estate from its ancestral roots to the futuristic skyline of urban development. His narrative, enriched with strategic frameworks and insightful analyses, serves as a compass for navigating the complex terrains of property ownership and investment. This seminal work, both enlightening and empowering, is a beacon for anyone aspiring to master the art and science of real estate in India."

CA Rishabh Kumar Sawansukha, Chairman JITO Centre for Excellence

"'Kagaz & Kabza' by Sanjjay Jain is an indispensable resource for anyone involved in the Indian real estate market. This book brilliantly encapsulates the complexities of property transactions through its comprehensive historical insights and the innovative KAGAZ and KABZA frameworks. Sanjjay's expertise shines throughout the book, as he offers actionable advice and strategic blueprints that are crucial for navigating legal and financial challenges in real estate. The frameworks introduced—KAGAZ for property documentation and KABZA for securing property rights—are especially valuable, providing readers with the tools needed to protect their investments. As a testament to Sanjjay's profound understanding of the market, I wholeheartedly recommend 'Kagaz & Kabza" to both newcomers and seasoned professionals looking to make informed decisions in Indian real estate."

Vikash Jain, Co-Founder - Share Samadhan Limited

"Let's be honest, at one point or another, every real estate investor has faced the dilemma of unclear paperwork or understanding the technical jargons behind title deeds. While grasping these nuances is crucial, very few resources provide clear and comprehensive guidance. Sanjjay Jain's 'Kagaz and Kabza' beautifully bridges this gap. This book is not merely a collection of information; it is a powerful tool that demystifies the complexities of property documentation and rights protection. Sanjjay Jain has crafted 'Kagaz and Kabza' with a visionary intent to empower readers—from first-time homebuyers to seasoned investors— by providing a deep understanding of the legal and procedural nuances of the Indian real estate market. The book introduces innovative frameworks like 'KAGAZ' for property documentation and 'KABZA' for safeguarding property rights, which are essential for anyone involved in real estate transactions. This book is a must-read for anyone looking to navigate the complexities of the Indian real estate landscape with confidence and strategic foresight."

Pradeep Chaudhary, Director - Multi Decor India Pvt Ltd

What Awaits You in Kagaz & Kabza

Welcome to the world of real estate, where every property has a story. 'Kagaz & Kabza' invites you to explore into the evolution of land and buildings in India, offering a fresh perspective on what makes a space a valuable asset. Discover how shifts in culture and economy shape the places we call home.

Chapter 1: Real Estate Evolution - Past, Present, Future

How did palatial estates evolve into the modern integrated townships and gated communities we see today? Journey through the architectural timeline of India and forecast the future trends that will shape our living and working spaces. Uncover the forces that transformed humble abodes into towering skyscrapers.

Chapter 2: Decoding the Indian Real Estate Ecosystem

What drives the market's heart to beat faster or slow down? We explore the intricate dance of supply and demand that determines property prices. explore into how migration trends and urban planning strategies are crucial factors in shaping market dynamics. Understand how government policies and global economic shifts play pivotal roles.

Chapter 3: KAGAZ - The Blueprint for Wise Property Documentation

The cornerstone of secure property ownership lies in its documentation. Discover the KAGAZ approach to ensure every piece of paper is your safeguard. Learn the significance of meticulous record-keeping and the impact of regulatory changes on property documentation. This method helps demystify the paperwork puzzle, ensuring your assets are protected.

Chapter 4: KABZA - Safeguarding Your Property Rights

Ownership is more than just having your name on a deed. Through the KABZA framework, learn how to assert and defend your property rights effectively. Explore strategies for dispute resolution and learn how to establish undisputed property boundaries. This framework guides you in navigating the legal landscape of real estate ownership.

Chapter 5: Strategic Mastery & Comprehensive Real Estate Navigator

Ready to turn knowledge into action? Discover how to strategically build and diversify your real estate portfolio to maximise returns and minimise risks. Learn about the advantages of eco-friendly investments and the financial benefits of understanding tax implications. This chapter equips you with advanced strategies for a robust investment approach.

Conclusion: The Path Forward in Real Estate

As you close this book, you'll be equipped not just with facts but with a framework to apply this knowledge effectively. Reflect on how you can use these insights to make informed decisions and shape your future in the real estate world. 'Kagaz & Kabza' isn't just about learning; it's about transforming knowledge into powerful actions.

Chapter 1

Real Estate Evolution - Past, Present, Future

Let's dive into India's fascinating real estate world. Here, every building holds a tale and each square foot captures a historical morsel and the country's hopes. I'm inviting you to join an exciting time-space adventure to discover India's real estate growth story. Our adventure splits into four interesting parts, each providing a distinct view of India's real estate transformation over time, still influencing the dreams of many.

Traditional Indian homes tell a compelling story of India's deep past, rich cultures and respect for nature. The design elements of courtyards, porches and open spaces symbolise more than aged architecture prowess. They reveal a longstanding value for community life. Let's journey together into the world of Indian home design, particularly the appeal and importance of courtyards and porches. Those of you in your 50s might recognise this, but for the younger crowd, it's set to be an exciting exploration.

1.1. The Allure of Traditional Indian Homes: Courtyards, Verandas and Family Bonds

Let's take a trip back to old Indian houses. In 'The Allure of Traditional Indian Homes: Courtyards, Verandas and Family Bonds', we enter classic buildings full of history. These houses, with sunlit courtyards and story-filled verandas, show the essence of Indian life. We reveal the design rules, cultural impact and ageless allure that still guide modern real estate.

1.2. Rising Skyline: Urban Landscape and the Shift to Gated Communities

As we fast forward to the present, 'Rising Skyline: Urban Landscape and the Shift to Gated Communities' paints a vivid picture of modern India. Here, the urban landscape reaches new heights, both literally and figuratively. Skyscrapers scrape the heavens and gated communities redefine the concept of urban living. We're exploring in this part how India's towns have changed and adapted to serve the shifting dreams, ways of life and requirements of people living there.

1.3. Real Estate Aspirations in India: Insights from Leading Moguls

In 'Real Estate Aspirations in India: Insights from Leading Moguls', we pause to listen to the wisdom of industry visionaries. These titans of real estate share their aspirations, strategies and commitment to innovation and sustainability. Their stories offer a unique glimpse into how real estate transcends mere business, becoming a force for positive change, community development and nation-building. This subchapter explores the heart and soul of India's real estate industry, where dreams of a brighter and better tomorrow are woven into the very fabric of urban landscapes.

1.4. Adapting to Post-COVID Living: Rediscovering Space and Sustainable Living

Our journey concludes with a visit to the post-pandemic world in 'Adapting to Post-COVID Living: Rediscovering Space and Sustainable Living'. Here, we witness the transformative impact of a global crisis on our homes and living spaces. The pandemic forced us to reimagine the essence of our dwellings, turning them into multifunctional sanctuaries where sustainability and eco-conscious living take centre stage. This subchapter underscores the resilience and adaptability of both individuals and the real estate industry in the face of adversity.

Get ready for an amazing journey through India's property landscape. Each subsection is filled with exciting tales, insights and discoveries.

Real estate in India is not just about bricks and mortar; it's a living testament to the nation's history, aspirations and innovation. Join us on this exhilarating journey, where the past, present and future of Indian real estate converge to create dreams, designs and destiny.

1.1. The Allure of Traditional Indian Homes: Courtyards, Verandas and Family Bonds

In the fast-paced world of real estate, with tall, shiny towers and the steady advancement of modern times, there's something valuable hidden. That valuable thing is the heart of old Indian homes. These homes still hold onto the sounds of history, reminding us of our deep cultural ties and the special connections we have with our environment.

Let's explore together. We'll check out courtyards, full of lasting beauty. We'll see verandas, always charming. We'll feel the strong ties made in these special homes.

Courtyards: Nature's Embrace and the Theater of Life

In the heart of old Indian houses, courtyards called 'Aangan' or 'Coura' exist. They're peaceful spots where nature's sounds and community life blend. They're not just parts of a building. They're alive with our customs and times, with history heard in the sounds of old trees' leaves.

> **"** *A house is made of bricks and beams.*
> *A home is made of hopes and dreams.*
> *- Unknown* **"**

Courtyards aren't just spaces; they are sanctuaries of culture, where festivals, rituals and celebrations find their stage. They exemplify oneness, with neighbours taking on familial roles and caring for one another as if they were relatives. Those who were previously unknown become steadfast mates, united by shared experiences and mutual care in the tight-knit neighbourhood. The residents, united in friendship, fully support one another, building long-lasting connections where strangers no longer exist.

Verandas: Guardians of Memories Through Time

Wrapped around the exteriors of traditional Indian homes like protective sentinels, verandas or 'jharokhas' stand as silent witnesses to the passage of time. These covered spaces, adorned with intricate designs and artistic detailing, are not just extensions; they are storytellers.

> **❝** *Architecture is a visual art and the buildings speak for themselves.*
> *- Julia Morgan* **❞**

Verandas offer more than just shelter from the elements; they provide solace, acting as a bridge between the sanctuary of home and the outside world. Here, one can savour the gentle breeze, sip a cup of tea or simply watch life unfold.

These spaces are where memories are etched into the very fabric of the home, where laughter resonates and where the present and past coexist in harmony.

Facts and Figures: An Empirical Perspective

Allow us to substantiate the significance of courtyards and verandas with empirical evidence. Studies have shown that such homes offer numerous advantages, including improved indoor air quality, enhanced thermal comfort and strengthened social connections.

Do you know about the 'Patwon Ki Haveli' in Jaisalmer?

In the heart of the Golden City of Jaisalmer, Rajasthan stands a true architectural gem that has withstood the sands of time for over two centuries. Patwon Ki Haveli, a cluster of five havelis, is not merely a structure but a living witness to the craftsmanship and design brilliance of its era.

Patwon Ki Haveli, dating back to the 18th century, offers a portal to bygone eras. Its sheer existence spans millennia, serving as a reminder of India's rich architectural past. The haveli, constructed by the Patwa family of traders, is a striking example of the opulence and artistic finesse that thrived in the region during this period.

The Oasis in the Desert: Rajasthan, known for its scorching desert landscapes, often demands architectural solutions that provide respite from the unforgiving sun. Patwon Ki Haveli does precisely that. Its cleverly designed courtyards serve as cool, shaded oases in the midst of the arid surroundings. These courtyards not only offer a retreat from the desert heat but also facilitate natural cross-ventilation throughout the complex, a remarkable feat of engineering that continues to inspire architects and engineers today.

As we dive deeper into the architectural marvel that is Patwon Ki Haveli, it's impossible to ignore the intricate jali work that adorns its verandas. Jali, a latticed screen, is not merely a decorative element but a functional one as well. The delicate patterns in the jali screens serve to filter the harsh sunlight, casting mesmerising patterns of light and shadow on the floors within. This play of light not only enhances the visual aesthetics but also moderates the indoor temperature, maintaining a comfortable environment even during the scorching summer months.

For instance, a study conducted by the Indian Green Building Council (IGBC) demonstrated that homes featuring courtyards experienced up to 50% lower indoor temperatures during the scorching summer months, significantly reducing the need for energy-intensive cooling systems. Moreover, individuals living in such homes reported lower instances of stress-related disorders, underscoring the profound impact of architectural design on overall well-being.

As we journey deeper into the allure of traditional Indian homes, it becomes apparent that these time-honoured abodes are not merely structures; they are living embodiments of culture, tradition and the enduring strength of family bonds. In an era where the real estate landscape is rapidly evolving, these homes serve as poignant reminders that certain traditions are worth preserving. Amidst the relentless march of modernity, the heartbeat of family and community remains steadfast.

Strengthening Family Bonds: The Beating Heart of Traditional Homes

Beyond the bricks and mortar, these homes are not just structures; they are the crucibles of family bonds, where generations unite, traditions thrive and familial togetherness is woven.

The Architecture of Togetherness: Traditional Indian homes are a symbol of thoughtful design that pays homage to the essence of community living. The very architecture of these homes is a celebration of familial togetherness. Courtyards and verandas, designed with meticulous care, serve as communal spaces where families come together to share their lives, joys and sorrows.

Grandparents as Pillars of Wisdom: In the heart of these traditional homes, grandparents are revered as the custodians of wisdom. Their presence is not just an addition but an integral part of the family structure. It's here that they share their life experiences, teach invaluable life lessons and become a living repository of cultural heritage.

Imagine a family residing in a centuries-old traditional home where the eldest member, Dadiji, sits under the shade of a centuries-old banyan tree in the courtyard. He imparts his wisdom to his grandchildren through stories, who listen with rapt attention. This passing down of wisdom, from one generation to another, is a living example of the magic that traditional homes foster.

Nurturing Dreams and Aspirations: For parents, these traditional homes become the nurturing grounds for dreams and aspirations. The sturdy walls of these homes witness children taking their first steps toward a promising future. The verandas, where family discussions take place, become the arenas where dreams are shared, goals are set and support is pledged.

Architecture that Encourages Social Interaction: The very layout of traditional homes encourages social interaction. These homes are not a collection of isolated rooms; they are a network of spaces that facilitate family gatherings, celebrations and the sharing of daily life. This design fortifies the ties that bind families together and this simple yet profound act of coming together fosters a sense of belonging and solidarity that modern homes often struggle to replicate.

Therefore, traditional Indian homes are more than just properties; they are the living embodiments of the values that define our culture. They are where love resides, where memories are created, where friends always belong and where laughter never ends. In these homes, the beating heart of family bonds grows stronger with each passing day.

As we continue our journey through the pages of 'Kagaz & Kabza', let us remember that property is not merely about ownership; it is about the stories, the traditions and the relationships that thrive within its walls. Traditional homes stand as proof of the enduring strength of family bonds and they inspire us to cherish these bonds in our own lives, no matter where we call home.

Another Perspective Regarding the Tradition: Joint Families and Their Influence on Indian Homes

In the diverse setup of Indian society, the traditional joint family system has intricately woven itself into the very fabric of property structures across the nation. Rooted in centuries-old cultural and religious practices, the joint family concept has not only left an indelible mark on architectural designs but has also fostered unique social dynamics that continue to shape Indian homes.

The roots of the joint family system in India stretch back to ancient cultural and religious practices that emphasise maintaining family unity, respecting elders and sharing resources. Historical accounts and scriptures bear proof to the prevalence of joint families in both royal households and common households alike.

These joint families exert a profound influence on property structures in various ways:

- **Larger Homes:** Joint families necessitate extensive living spaces capable of accommodating multiple generations, including grandparents, parents, children and sometimes even aunts, uncles and cousins. This often results in larger properties or homes with multiple units within a single structure.

- **Shared Spaces:** Emphasising shared living spaces, joint families create common areas for gatherings, dining and communal activities. These shared spaces are thoughtfully designed to promote family bonding and interactions, significantly influencing the layout and design of the property.

- **Privacy Considerations:** While joint families foster togetherness, they also value individual privacy. Property designs frequently incorporate separate wings or sections to ensure privacy for different generations or branches of the family.

- **Flexibility and Expansion:** Property structures within joint families are inherently flexible, accommodating the changing needs of the family. This flexibility allows for easy expansion or modification of living areas as new members join the family through marriages or births.

- **Family Heritage:** Joint families often attach significant value to preserving family traditions and cultural heritage within the property. This influence manifests in the design and layout, which may include dedicated spaces for religious rituals, memorabilia or cultural practices.

- **Economic Considerations:** Joint families often pool their resources for property acquisition and maintenance. This collective approach can significantly impact property decisions, such as choosing a location convenient for all family members.

- **Unity and Bonding:** Property structures within joint families foster unity and strong family bonds. They enable daily interactions, shared responsibilities and a close-knit environment that nurtures a profound sense of belonging.

One prominent example is the 'Nalukettu' houses of Kerala. These traditional homes feature interconnected rooms surrounding a central courtyard. This design offers segregated living quarters for different branches of the family while facilitating communal activities in the central space. The 'Havelis' of Rajasthan similarly showcase intricate architecture that enables joint families to coexist harmoniously.

The Nalukettu Houses of Kerala

The 'Nalukettu' houses stand as an exemplar of architectural ingenuity tailored to accommodate joint families. Comprising four wings, each designated for a different generation, these houses symbolise the essence of togetherness. The interconnectedness of the wings fosters family unity, while the courtyard serves as a hub for ceremonies and social interactions. Remarkably, the design not only strengthens emotional bonds but also promotes sustainable living through natural ventilation and lighting, reducing energy consumption, as revealed by a study conducted by the Indian Institute of Technology (IIT) Kharagpur.

Socio-Cultural Impacts: Redefining Property Ownership and Gender Equality

The joint family system has left an indelible mark on Indian society, reshaping property ownership norms, inheritance patterns and decision-making processes. The concept of 'coparcenary', where ancestral property is jointly held, has been a foundational principle governing property ownership in joint families.

The term 'coparcener' denotes a 'Joint Heir' in a Hindu Undivided Family (HUF) who shares legal rights for inheriting property, title and money as defined under Hindu Succession Laws. This person has the authority to demand property partition. Notably, all coparceners are HUF members, though not all HUF members may be coparceners.

Challenges and Changing Trends: Adapting to Modern Realities

While the joint family system has brought about numerous positive changes, evolving societal dynamics, urbanisation and economic factors have ushered in a shift toward nuclear families and alternative property structures. Rapid urban development has given rise to apartment complexes and gated communities, where individual ownership often takes precedence over joint ownership.

The influences of joint families on property structures in India have carved an enduring legacy, leaving an indelible mark on architectural

> In a landmark 2020 ruling, the Supreme Court of India upheld equal coparceny rights for daughters in ancestral property, regardless of their marital status. This groundbreaking judgement marked a significant stride toward gender equality in property ownership, challenging age-old biases against women's inheritance rights. As per the National Crime Records Bureau (NCRB), this legal transformation is gradually reshaping the property landscape, promoting financial independence among women.

designs, property ownership norms and family dynamics. The 'Nalukettu' houses and coparcenary rights serve as emblematic symbols of this influence, reflecting the harmonious coexistence of generations and the evolving concept of property ownership.

While changing trends present challenges to the traditional joint family system, its impact on property structures continues to be a compelling aspect of Indian culture and society.

1.2. Rising Skyline: Urban Landscape and the Shift to Gated Communities

The Indian Urban Landscape is currently undergoing a breathtaking transformation. Our cities, which once sprawled endlessly in every direction, have now cast their gaze skyward to accommodate the lofty aspirations of millions. The proliferation of towering skyscrapers, architectural marvels and cutting-edge residential complexes paints a vivid tableau of urban living in the 21st century.

This transformation is more than just a change in physical appearance; it's a reflection of evolving lifestyles, dreams and the inexorable allure of urban life. The city, with its tantalising promise of opportunities, connectivity and convenience, is redefining how we perceive and experience urban living.

The Rise of Gated Communities: Urban Sanctuaries

In the middle of this impressive vertical growth, another amazing thing is happening—the increase in gated communities. These self-contained havens blend smoothly into the busy city life, providing a special mix of exclusivity and community living. This introduces a fresh aspect to urban living.

> **"** *Home is the place where, when you have to go there, they have to take you in.*
> *- Robert Frost* **"**

Gated communities transcend the conventional notion of housing; they are meticulously designed masterpieces of urban planning and architecture. Within these gated precincts, lushly landscaped gardens unfurl, state-of-the-art amenities beckon and an omnipresent sense of security prevails. Often guarded by vigilant sentinels, they extend an oasis of tranquillity amidst the urban cacophony.

People are drawn to gated communities because they promise a better way of living. It's a big change in how people live, seeking more order in the chaos of city life. In these areas, residents enjoy peaceful green spaces, join in community activities and feel safe with constant security.

> *The joy of brightening other lives, bearing each other's burdens, easing other's loads and supplanting empty hearts and lives with generous gifts becomes for us the magic of the holidays.*
>
> *- W.C. Jones*

Moreover, these communities cultivate a deep sense of belonging and camaraderie among residents. Neighbours effortlessly evolve into lifelong friends, while shared spaces seamlessly transform into vibrant venues for celebrations and social gatherings. It's a lifestyle that transcends the confines of traditional urban living; it's a vibrant community where bonds are forged and dreams are nurtured.

Case Study: Gated Communities in Gurugram - DLF The Camellias

Image source: stirworld.com (https://www.stirworld.com/see-features-dlf-camellias-in-gurugram-redefines-luxury-urban-living-for-contemporary-india)

Gurugram, a bustling hub in the National Capital Region, epitomises the transformation in modern living. Gated communities like DLF The Camellias Arch redefine luxury and convenience. The Camellias offers a lavish lifestyle with its exquisite residences, landscaped gardens, recreational and sports facilities. These developments highlight how Gurugram is at the forefront of providing an elevated living experience.

Gurugram's rapid ascent as a premium destination for gated communities underscores the evolution of urban living in India. The city, known for its corporate corridors and bustling lifestyle, is now synonymous with opulent living spaces that cater to the desires and aspirations of urbanites.

In the centre of Gurugram, DLF The Camellias is a symbol of luxury and elegance. This gated community sets a new standard for luxury living with its grand apartments, well-kept gardens and a variety of amenities. People living here aren't just homeowners; they are keepers of a lifestyle that blends sophistication with comfort. The Camellias is more than just a place to live; it embodies aspirations, a place where the art of refined living is embraced every day.

This success story of the gated community in Gurugram is not just about lavish living; it is a narrative of urban dreams realised. This epitomises the changing face of urban living, where convenience, luxury and community converge to create an aspirational lifestyle.

Facts and Figures: The Gated Community Revolution

The rise of gated communities isn't a fleeting trend; it mirrors the dynamic shift in urban living. According to a comprehensive report by ANAROCK Property Consultants, over 67% of residential launches in Gurugram in a given period were in the form of apartments. The Haryana government's focus on infrastructure development and connectivity has further contributed to Gurugram's status as a preferred location for gated community living.

The surge in demand for gated communities isn't restricted to Gurugram alone. Across major cities in India, there has been a discernible shift in the preference for community living. Urbanites are increasingly seeking the safety, community and amenities that these developments offer. The notion of security, both physical and emotional, plays a pivotal role in the choice of gated communities. Families find solace in the fact that their loved ones can thrive in a secure and nurturing environment.

Gated communities are also quick to adapt to the changing preferences of urban dwellers. Today, these enclaves are designed not just for living but for experiencing life. From clubhouses that host a myriad of activities to fitness centres equipped with state-of-the-art equipment, developers are crafting lifestyle destinations within the city.

With environmental concerns gaining prominence, developers in Gurugram are incorporating sustainable practices in their projects. From energy-efficient designs to waste management systems, these gated communities are aligning with the global push for eco-friendly living. The inclusion of green spaces, rainwater harvesting systems and solar power integration reflects a commitment to sustainable urbanisation.

Sustainability isn't just a buzzword; it's a guiding principle that influences every aspect of these developments. The emphasis on eco-friendly living isn't just about conserving resources; it's about fostering a healthier and more harmonious way of life.

Therefore, in a rapidly evolving urban landscape, apartments and gated communities have emerged as the vanguard of modern living in India. The case of Gurugram exemplifies how these developments cater to diverse lifestyle preferences while encapsulating security, convenience and community. As urbanisation continues, the popularity of such housing options is expected to grow, reshaping the concept of residential living in the country.

As we conclude this exploration of India's changing urban landscape, from the rising skyline to the flourishing gated communities, it becomes evident that the evolution of real estate is a multifaceted journey. The allure of vertical living and the rise of gated communities encapsulate the changing aspirations of urban India, where convenience, security and community converge to redefine the concept of home.

This transformation is not just about physical structures but also about the dreams and lifestyles they enable. It's a confirmation of the dynamic nature of the real estate sector and its ability to adapt to the evolving needs of the populace.

Now, let's shift our focus from the evolving city landscape to the ambitious dreams of India's top real estate tycoons. Their perspectives guide the way in this ever-changing industry. These aspirations go beyond physical buildings, delving into community creation, sustainable development and the core elements that turn a house into a home.

1.3. Real Estate Aspirations in India: Insights from Leading Moguls

The real estate scene in India has undergone significant changes, thanks to the influence of visionaries and industry leaders. This section explores the dreams and perspectives of key figures in the Indian real estate sector. Although we might not have access to specific articles or interviews, we rely on general knowledge and public statements made by notable personalities in the field.

India's real estate sector has come a long way, riding on the waves of urbanisation, changing demographics and economic growth. Central to this evolution have been the luminaries of the real estate realm. Icons like Hiranandani's, DLF's, Godrej's, TATA's, Mahindra's and others have been instrumental in defining the industry's course.

Key Aspirations and Insights:

1. **Sustainable Development:** Sustainability plays a central role in the aspirations of several influential figures in the Indian real estate sector. In an age characterised by environmental awareness and concerns about climate change, leaders like Anand Mahindra, Chairman of the Mahindra Group, advocate for sustainable practices in real estate. Their vision goes beyond mere financial gains, reflecting a dedication to the well-being of the planet and the prosperity of future generations.

   Anand Mahindra's words echo this sentiment: "We must build not just for today but for the world we want to leave behind."

Incorporating eco-friendly construction materials, renewable energy sources and waste reduction initiatives are some ways these industry leaders translate their environmental aspirations into tangible actions.

2. **Affordable Housing:** At the heart of Tata Value Homes' philosophy lies a simple yet profound vision: to make homeownership a reality for countless Indians who dream of having a place they can call their own. This vision aligns perfectly with the ethos of the Tata Group, one of India's oldest and most respected conglomerates known for its commitment to social responsibility and nation-building.

> ❝ *Our vision for Tata Value Homes is to provide affordable housing solutions to all and create a positive and lasting impact on society. We believe that a home is not just a structure; it's a place where dreams take shape and lives are transformed.*
>
> *- Brotin Banerjee, Managing Director and CEO, Tata Housing Development Company Ltd.* ❞

3. **Technology and Innovation:** Innovation is the lifeblood of progress in the real estate sector. Leading figures in the industry recognise that embracing technology is essential for staying relevant and competitive. Niranjan Hiranandani, a titan in the Indian real estate landscape, champions the adoption of technology and innovation to streamline operations and enhance customer experiences.

Hiranandani states, "Innovation isn't an option; it's a necessity. We must harness technology to create better homes and experiences."

Digital marketing, tech solutions and smart home integration are some areas where innovation is visibly reshaping the industry. These innovations not only improve efficiency but also cater to the evolving preferences of tech-savvy homebuyers.

4. **Global Expansion:** Ambitious leaders of the Indian real estate sector harbour aspirations beyond the nation's borders. The vision includes establishing a global footprint, diversifying portfolios and tapping into international markets. Adi Godrej, Chairman of the Godrej Group, is one such visionary.

Godrej's words reflect this global outlook: "Our journey doesn't end at the horizon; it extends across continents."

Expanding globally isn't merely about geographic expansion; it's about exploring new opportunities, forming international partnerships and bringing India's real estate prowess to a global audience.

5. **Community Development:** Beyond bricks and mortar, leading moguls aspire to create vibrant, integrated communities. These communities are designed to offer a high quality of life, fostering a sense of belonging and harmony among residents. The idea is to move beyond just selling properties to curating holistic lifestyles.

"Building homes is just the beginning; building communities is our ultimate aspiration," emphasises a spokesperson from a leading real estate conglomerate.

Amenities, green spaces and cultural initiatives are integral to this aspiration. The aim is to create spaces where families thrive, children play and neighbours become friends.

6. **Challenges and Resilience:** The Indian real estate sector is no stranger to challenges. Regulatory hurdles, funding constraints and market fluctuations are par for the course. What distinguishes these influential figures is their resilience and ability to adapt to challenging situations. They demonstrate the skill to innovate and adjust to market changes, showcasing strong leadership qualities.

7. **Navigating Regulatory Complexities:** The Indian real estate sector has faced a significant challenge in navigating the intricate maze of regulatory complexities. The implementation of the Real

Estate Regulation and Development Act (RERA) in 2016 marked a watershed moment. RERA sought to bring transparency and accountability to the sector, making it imperative for developers to register their projects and adhere to stringent guidelines.

Moguls like Niranjan Hiranandani, Chairman of the Hiranandani Group, have not only embraced such reforms but also voiced their endorsement, viewing them as necessary steps to boost consumer confidence and encourage responsible development. They recognise that these regulations, although demanding, are pivotal in restoring faith in the sector, which had been marred by delays and unscrupulous practices.

Hiranandani states, "Regulatory reforms, such as RERA, are crucial to instil trust in the real estate sector. It's an opportunity for developers to demonstrate their commitment to quality and timely delivery."

By supporting and complying with these regulatory reforms, industry leaders are not merely demonstrating their adaptability but also championing a culture of transparency and accountability that benefits all stakeholders.

8. **Financial Prudence**: Access to funding and managing financial resources efficiently is critical in the real estate sector. The ability to secure funds at competitive rates and deploy them judiciously is a key challenge. Leaders like Adi Godrej, Chairman of the Godrej Group, have showcased financial prudence in managing their real estate empires, ensuring sustainable growth even in volatile economic conditions.

   The financial prudence exercised by these industry giants extends to risk management, diversification of portfolios and maintaining a healthy debt-equity ratio. Such measures act as a bulwark against economic downturns, ensuring that their organisations remain resilient in the face of adversity.

Adi Godrej's approach exemplifies this financial astuteness: "A well-diversified portfolio is our strategy for navigating market uncertainties. We're committed to ensuring the financial health of our real estate ventures."

Their ability to secure funding at favourable terms and wisely allocate resources underscores their strategic prowess and long-term vision, enabling them to weather economic storms.

9. **Market Volatility:** The real estate market is susceptible to economic fluctuations, interest rate changes and shifts in market sentiment. Visionaries in the industry closely monitor these variables and adapt their strategies accordingly. Rajiv Singh, Chairman of DLF, has demonstrated remarkable strategic agility in navigating market volatility.

Singh emphasises, "Flexibility is our strength. We're attuned to the market's pulse and ready to pivot as needed."

In practice, this means diversifying offerings, exploring emerging markets and responding swiftly to changing consumer preferences. These leaders understand that the real estate sector is intrinsically linked to the broader economy and they adapt their strategies to align with prevailing economic conditions.

Their market foresight and willingness to embrace change not only shield their organisations from downturns but also position them to capitalise on emerging opportunities. This dynamic approach underscores their ability to thrive amidst market turbulence.

The dreams and perspectives of key figures in the Indian real estate industry offer a glimpse into a dynamic and forward-thinking sector. Their visions go beyond mere profit; they embody a dedication to sustainability, inclusivity, innovation and community development.

As these influential individuals continue to mould India's urban landscape, their aspirations are likely to shape the industry's future for generations.

The evolution of Indian real estate is an ongoing saga and the aspirations of these moguls continue to fuel its transformation. While the challenges are significant, the resilience and visionary outlook of these leaders suggest that the future of Indian real estate is poised for brilliance.

Their ability to navigate regulatory complexities, exercise financial prudence and adapt to market volatility are affirmations of their leadership. These leaders serve as symbols of resilience in a continually changing sector, epitomising the spirit of innovation and progress that characterises the Indian real estate landscape.

As we wrap up our examination of the dreams and perspectives of key figures in the Indian real estate industry, it's clear that their visionary approach and dedication to innovation will persist in shaping the urban landscape of India. However, in a world forever altered by the COVID-19 pandemic, their thoughts, visions and plans have evolved to meet the changing needs and aspirations of a post-pandemic society. The real estate moguls we have explored are not just champions of profitability but also of sustainability, inclusivity, innovation and community development.

1.4. Adapting to Post-COVID Living: Rediscovering Space and Sustainable Living

In the aftermath of the unprecedented challenges brought about by the COVID-19 pandemic, the real estate landscape in India and globally has undergone a significant transformation. This change goes beyond the strategies and ambitions of industry leaders; it deeply influences how we perceive and engage with our living spaces. In this section, we explore how the thoughts, visions and plans of builders, buyers and investors have been markedly affected and reshaped by the pandemic. The seismic disruptions caused by COVID-19 have prompted a collective reassessment of what defines a home, which features are essential and how we can lead more sustainable and adaptable lives in the face of unexpected global challenges.

A Global Pandemic and Real Estate's Evolution:

The COVID-19 pandemic left an indelible mark on our lives, challenging every facet of our existence, including how we perceive and utilise our living spaces. With remote work becoming the new norm and our homes transforming into multipurpose sanctuaries, the real estate industry found itself at the forefront of a paradigm shift.

The pandemic was a wake-up call for us all, forcing us to reimagine the very essence of our homes. They are no longer mere shelters; they've become our offices, gyms, classrooms and retreats. In response to this profound shift, our homes are evolving to accommodate these diverse roles, sparking a revolution in real estate design and functionality.

The Rediscovery of Space: Quality Over Quantity

As the pandemic unfolded, a profound realisation dawned – bigger homes don't necessarily equate to better living. Instead, the focus shifted toward optimising space for multifunctionality. Homebuyers began to prioritise quality over quantity, seeking layouts that could adapt to evolving needs.

This demand for adaptable spaces led architects and developers to create designs that allow rooms to seamlessly transform. Dining areas now double as home offices, balconies serve as yoga studios and living rooms are adaptable for virtual gatherings. The evolution of space design reflects our determination to find opportunity amid adversity.

Sustainable Living: The New Imperative

The pandemic amplified our awareness of our impact on the environment. As we spent more time at home, we became increasingly conscious of our ecological footprint. Sustainable living became not just an option but an imperative for those seeking harmony with nature.

Green real estate solutions gained momentum, with homebuyers opting for eco-friendly developments. These forward-thinking communities prioritise energy conservation, waste reduction and green spaces. Solar panels, rainwater harvesting systems and green roofs are becoming standard features in modern homes, aligning with the global shift toward sustainability.

Stories of Adaptation: Real Impact in Real Lives

To illustrate the real impact of this transformation, let's explore into a story.

The Singhs, a family of four residing in the bustling heart of Delhi, found themselves facing an unexpected dilemma as the COVID-19 pandemic swept across the nation. The confines of their cramped apartment, which had once been their cosy abode, suddenly transformed into a challenge they hadn't anticipated. With both Mr and Mrs Singh working remotely and their children attending online classes, the limited space in their home became increasingly restrictive. The lack of a designated workspace and the constant jostling for quiet corners for virtual meetings and classes added to their daily stress.

As the months wore on, it became abundantly clear to the Singhs that their living situation needed to change. They yearned for a more spacious and accommodating environment, one that would not only meet their immediate needs but also align with their newfound commitment to sustainability. The pandemic had not only reshaped their work and lifestyle preferences but also heightened their awareness of their ecological footprint.

The problem was clear: the Singhs needed a new home that offered ample space for remote work and virtual learning, as well as eco-conscious features that resonated with their growing environmental consciousness.

Their solution came in the form of a vibrant and eco-conscious apartment complex located in a quieter neighbourhood on the outskirts of Delhi. This meticulously planned community was designed to provide residents with a harmonious blend of modern living and sustainable practices.

The Singhs were enchanted by the abundant greenery surrounding the complex, forming a peaceful oasis amidst the bustling city. It was a stark contrast to the crowded streets they were used to. The complex featured solar panels on the rooftops, utilising the sun's power to produce clean and renewable energy. This dedication to green energy perfectly matched the Singhs' desire for a sustainable lifestyle.

One of the highlights of their newfound home was the community garden, a vibrant space where residents could bond over gardening and collectively contribute to reducing their carbon footprint. The garden not only provided a therapeutic escape from the stresses of daily life but also served as an attestation to the community's dedication to sustainable living.

For the Singhs, this move was transformative. The spacious layout of their new apartment provided dedicated workspaces for both Mr and Mrs Singh, allowing them to work efficiently without encroaching on each other's domains. Their children were delighted to have their own rooms for virtual classes, fostering an environment conducive to learning.

More than just a change of address, their decision to move to this eco-conscious apartment complex improved their quality of life immeasurably. The Singhs found themselves embracing a sustainable lifestyle more wholeheartedly than ever before. The clean energy generated by solar panels reduced their reliance on non-renewable sources and significantly lowered their electricity bills.

With the community garden as their playground, the Singhs not only cultivated a love for gardening but also forged strong bonds with their neighbours. It was no longer just a place to live; it was a thriving community, a place they were proud to call home.

Their journey exemplified how the pandemic had not only compelled them to redefine their living space but also to make a conscious choice toward sustainability. It was a decision that not only improved their immediate quality of life but also contributed to a greener, more eco-conscious future—a future they were excited to be a part of.

As we conclude our journey through the realms of post-COVID living, one thing is clear – real estate is more than an industry; it's a reflection of our evolving needs and aspirations. Our homes have transformed into adaptable sanctuaries and sustainable havens, guiding us toward a brighter, more resilient future.

Beyond the Pandemic: A Glimpse into the Future

The pandemic may have brought uncertainty, but it has also sparked innovation and a renewed focus on what truly matters in our homes. The path ahead is one of adaptation, where the real estate industry will play a pivotal role in shaping a future that is resilient, sustainable and harmonious with our evolving world.

Fact: According to a report by Anarock Property Consultants, remote work is expected to increase the demand for larger homes in India, with a preference for properties that offer extra space for home offices and study areas.

In this rapidly evolving landscape, it's essential to recognise that the changes brought about by the pandemic are not temporary; they are shaping the future of real estate. With remote work likely to remain a significant part of our lives, the concept of home as a multifunctional space is here to stay.

Fact: A survey conducted by Knight Frank India in 2021 revealed that 69% of respondents are willing to pay a premium for properties that offer better amenities and flexible spaces suitable for remote working.

This shift is influencing architectural designs, interior layouts and the incorporation of technology. Homes are being designed with flexibility in mind, allowing residents to seamlessly switch between work, leisure and family activities. Designers and developers are collaborating to create homes that truly cater to the needs of the modern family.

Fact: According to a report by JLL India, there has been a 30% increase in demand for wellness-oriented residential projects that incorporate green building standards, improved ventilation and open spaces post-pandemic.

These changes are not just about comfort and convenience; they are about creating living environments that support our evolving lifestyles and priorities. As we continue to navigate the post-pandemic world, the real estate industry will play a crucial role in providing solutions that enhance the quality of life for individuals and families alike.

Sustainable Living: The New Norm

The pandemic has heightened our awareness of environmental issues and sustainability. Homebuyers are now actively seeking properties that incorporate eco-friendly features. This demand has led to a surge in green real estate developments.

Builders and developers are focusing on energy-efficient designs, the use of renewable energy sources, water conservation systems and waste management solutions. These eco-conscious features not only reduce the environmental impact of properties but also result in long-term cost savings for residents.

The Rise of Suburban Living:

Another notable trend in post-pandemic real estate is the resurgence of suburban living. The lockdowns and remote work options have prompted many urban residents to reconsider their living arrangements. Suburbs and smaller towns are gaining popularity as people seek larger homes with outdoor spaces.

The Future of Co-working Spaces:

While remote work has become the new normal, the need for physical office spaces has not disappeared entirely. However, the new role of office spaces is evolving. Many companies are now exploring flexible co-working arrangements that allow employees to work from satellite offices closer to their homes.

These co-working spaces offer the benefits of a professional work environment without the need for a long commute. They provide an excellent solution for those who want to maintain a work-life balance while enjoying the advantages of office facilities.

Therefore, the post-COVID real estate landscape in India is a dynamic one, shaped by changing lifestyles, technological advancements and a growing emphasis on sustainability. As we adapt to the new normal, our homes are evolving to meet our multifaceted needs and the real estate industry is at the forefront of this transformation.

As we look to the future, one thing is certain – our homes will continue to be our sanctuaries, offering comfort, functionality and sustainability. The real estate industry in India is embracing these changes and developers have to be committed to creating homes that cater to the needs of the modern Indian family. Whether it's the integration of technology, the focus on sustainability or the resurgence of suburban living, these trends will shape the future of real estate in India for years to come. So, as you embark on your real estate journey, consider how these trends align with your lifestyle and aspirations and make informed decisions that will shape your future in a rapidly changing world.

"As we look to the future, let us remember that real estate is not just about structures but about the dreams they house. From the foundations of ancient abodes to the pinnacles of modern skylines, each brick and beam tells a story of evolution, ambition and the relentless pursuit of excellence."

Chapter 2

Decoding the Indian Real Estate Ecosystem

In this chapter, we explore an enlightening and immersive journey to unravel the complexities of the Indian real estate ecosystem. Our aim is to provide you with a thorough understanding of the intricate workings of the Indian real estate sector. Whether you are a first-time homebuyer, a seasoned property investor or simply someone curious about India's real estate market, this chapter will provide you with the knowledge and insights necessary to navigate this dynamic and ever-evolving landscape.

The real estate business in India is a dynamic mosaic woven from several threads, each shaped by the interaction of history, culture, economy and geography. Within this vast canvas, you'll find a broad range of real estate offers, ranging from traditional village houses to towering skyscrapers that decorate the skylines of dynamic urban centres. The purpose of this chapter is to shed light on the intricate web that is India's real estate market, allowing you to appreciate the industry's depth and complexity.

As we explore into the various facets of India's real estate landscape, you'll gain insights into the unique characteristics that define each segment, the challenges and opportunities they present and the key factors influencing the decisions of buyers, sellers and investors. By the end of this chapter, you'll be better equipped to navigate the Indian real estate market with confidence, armed with knowledge that spans from the grassroots to the skyscrapers that grace our cities.

Let us begin this engaging voyage by unravelling the threads of India's real estate, learning about its rich history, the various housing options available and the road map for buyers and sellers in this fascinating market.

2.1. The Indian Real Estate Panorama: An In-Depth Analysis

To truly appreciate the Indian real estate ecosystem, we must walk on a comprehensive journey that probes even deeper into its various dimensions. The Indian real estate sector is a complex and dynamic field that has undergone significant transformation over the years. Buckle up as we take you on an immersive exploration of India's real estate.

Historical Perspective:

Imagine standing in the heart of India's historical city of Jaipur, commonly known as the 'Pink City'. The city's nickname comes from its radiant terracotta-coloured buildings, a tribute to its rich history and unique urban planning. Founded in 1727 by Maharaja Sawai Jai Singh II, Jaipur was meticulously designed with wide streets, well-organised markets and awe-inspiring palaces.

Jaipur's architecture showcases the fusion of traditional Rajput and Mughal styles, making it a living testimony to India's architectural heritage. This historical perspective reminds us that India's real estate story is not just about bricks and mortar but also about culture, tradition and vision.

Jaipur is just one example of India's architectural marvels. Across the country, you can find structures like the ancient caves of Ajanta and Ellora, the stunning stepwells of Gujarat and the majestic forts of Rajasthan. Each of these architectural wonders tells a story, reflecting the historical, cultural and economic dynamics of their times.

Understanding this historical perspective is akin to taking a journey through time, where we witness the evolution of real estate from humble beginnings to grandeur. It allows us to appreciate how architectural styles, construction techniques and urban planning principles have evolved over centuries to shape the modern landscape.

Urban Vs. Rural Real Estate:

The division between urban and rural real estate in India is like exploring two distinct worlds within the same country. On one hand, we have the bustling urban areas with their modern amenities, towering skyscrapers and luxury properties. These urban spaces are the engines of economic growth, attracting professionals, entrepreneurs and investors from all corners of the globe.

For instance, Mumbai, India's financial capital, is not just a city; it's a living testimony to the Indian dream. Its skyline, adorned with architectural marvels like the Bandra-Worli Sea Link and luxury high-rises, showcases the city's ambition and progress. Mumbai's real estate market, a mix of traditional chawls and futuristic high-rises, offers something for everyone. It's a place where dreams are born and fortunes are made.

On the other hand, rural India paints a different picture. Here, the real estate landscape is shaped by agrarian traditions that have sustained communities for generations. Villages and small towns are home to a diverse array of housing styles, ranging from humble mud huts to sprawling farmhouses. These regions reflect the rich rural life, where land is not just an asset but a way of life.

Understanding the urban-rural divide is not just a matter of geography; it's a lens through which we can examine the economic, social and cultural diversity of India. It's a reminder that the real estate sector isn't a monolith; it's a kaleidoscope of experiences and opportunities.

Socioeconomic Factors:

Real estate in India is not just about properties; it's about people, aspirations and the dynamics of a rapidly evolving society. Socioeconomic factors play a pivotal role in shaping the real estate landscape and understanding them is like deciphering the DNA of India's property market.

Consider the rise of IT hubs like Bengaluru and Hyderabad. These cities have transformed into technological powerhouses, attracting a young and dynamic workforce seeking job opportunities. The influx of professionals into these cities has not only fueled the demand for housing but has also led to a surge in commercial real estate. The rapid growth of these urban centres is a reflection of India's aspirations to become a global technology hub.

But it's not just about big cities. Smaller towns and emerging urban clusters are also making their mark on India's real estate map. As industries diversify and government initiatives promote inclusive growth, these regions are witnessing a surge in infrastructure development and property investment. This dynamic landscape ensures that real estate isn't limited to a few megacities but is spread across the country, offering diverse opportunities.

Regulatory Environment:

Navigating the Indian real estate sector involves understanding the rules of the game and in recent years, the rules have changed significantly. The Real Estate (Regulation and Development) Act, of 2016 (RERA) was a game-changer that brought transparency and accountability to the industry.

RERA empowered buyers and investors by ensuring that developers adhere to timelines, disclose project details and meet quality standards. This regulatory framework has instilled confidence in the market, making it more buyer-friendly. It has transformed real estate from being an opaque, risky venture into a transparent and secure investment option.

Understanding the regulatory environment is like having a compass in a dense forest; it helps you navigate the complexities of the real estate market, ensuring that your investments are protected and your rights as a buyer are upheld.

Market Size and Growth:

India's real estate market is a behemoth in its own right. According to reports from the National Real Estate Development Council (NAREDCO), it contributes significantly to the country's GDP and employment. The sector's consistent growth, despite occasional fluctuations, makes it a compelling investment option.

The market size and growth trends can vary significantly depending on the region, segment and economic factors. For instance, the residential real estate market may experience different trends compared to the commercial or industrial sectors. It's crucial to stay updated with the latest statistics and market dynamics to make informed decisions.

The real estate scene in India is always changing, like a painting that gets more beautiful with each new development. To do well in this field, you have to be quick, knowledgeable and think ahead. It's not just about buying and selling properties; it's about understanding the pulse of a nation, the dreams of its people and the potential of its future.

In the upcoming subparts of this chapter, we will explore various aspects of India's real estate ecosystem, ranging from housing varieties and investment insights to the impact of technological transformation and eco-friendly development practices. Each subpart will provide valuable insights, case studies and actionable knowledge tailored to empower readers in their real estate journey.

Now that we have taken a deeper dive into the Indian real estate panorama, let's move forward and explore the diverse housing varieties that define India's real estate landscape.

2.2. Housing Varieties in India: From Grassroots to Skyscrapers

"In real estate, location isn't just about geography; it's about your life's landscape."

Welcome to the second subchapter of 'Kagaz & Kabza: Decoding the Indian Real Estate Ecosystem'. In this journey of discovery, we've laid the foundation by understanding the historical and socioeconomic context of the Indian real estate ecosystem. Now, let's take a deeper dive into the fascinating world of housing varieties that make up the diverse tapestry of India's real estate landscape.

A Kaleidoscope of Architectural Styles:

India's housing varieties are a reflection of its rich and multifaceted culture, history and geography. As we explore, keep in mind that every structure, whether humble or grand, tells a unique story about the people who inhabit it, the region it stands in and the traditions it upholds.

1. Traditional Village Dwellings: A Glimpse into Rural Life

Our journey begins in the heart of rural India, where the essence of the country resides. Traditional village dwellings offer a window into a way of life deeply rooted in agrarian traditions. These simple yet functional structures, often made of mud and thatch, paint a vivid picture of rural existence.

Mud houses with thatched roofs, embellished with vibrant wall paintings, are a common sight in rural areas. These homes are an example of the ingenuity of rural communities, as they use locally sourced materials to create dwellings that are not only sustainable but also resilient against the elements.

One exemplary architectural form is the 'bhunga' of Kutch, Gujarat. These circular huts, crafted from natural materials found in the region, are more than just homes; they are an example of sustainable living in harmony with nature. The unique design of bhungas helps maintain comfortable indoor temperatures during the extreme weather conditions of the arid region. It is a declaration of how indigenous wisdom continues to shape the architectural landscape of India.

Traditional village dwellings are not only a representation of rural architecture but also a symbol of the close-knit communities that thrive in these areas. As you explore the country's villages, you'll encounter architectural styles, each unique to its region and steeped in local tradition.

2. Charming Colonial Bungalows: Echoes of the Past

The colonial era left an indelible mark on India's architectural landscape and perhaps nowhere is this more evident than in the charming colonial bungalows that still grace various parts of the country. These spacious, single-story homes are characterised by their large verandas, sloping roofs and well-manicured gardens, all of which bear the unmistakable influence of British architecture.

As we trace the footsteps of history, a stroll through the leafy suburbs of Kolkata offers a glimpse of these architectural gems. Colonial bungalows, lovingly preserved and maintained, stand as living reminders of a bygone era. These homes are more than just structures; they are portals to a time when India's urban landscape began to evolve.

3. Urban Apartments: Modern Living Redefined

As we transition from the countryside to India's bustling urban centres, the landscape undergoes a transformation. Here, the skyline is defined by a forest of high-rises and apartment complexes. Urbanisation has ushered in a new era of modern apartment living characterised by convenience and luxury.

Mumbai, often referred to as the 'City of Dreams', boasts a skyline adorned with towering residential complexes that seem to touch the heavens. These apartments offer breathtaking views of the Arabian Sea and world-class amenities that cater to the aspirations of the urban elite. Mumbai's real estate market is a vibrant blend of traditional chawls and futuristic high-rises and it embodies the city's ceaseless growth and ambition.

In Bengaluru, the Silicon Valley of India, modern apartment living has become synonymous with the city's tech-savvy population. Apartments here are equipped with state-of-the-art amenities, catering to the needs of young professionals and families alike. It's a reflection of how urban India is redefining the concept of contemporary living.

4. Historic Havelis: Architectural Grandeur Unveiled

In the heart of Rajasthan, you'll encounter another architectural marvel – the haveli. These historic mansions are known for their grandeur, intricate carvings and sprawling courtyards. Havelis serve as a testamentary to the opulence of India's merchant class during eras gone by.

Shekhawati, often referred to as the 'Open-Air Art Gallery of Rajasthan', is a treasure trove of havelis. These majestic structures, adorned with frescoes and ornate architecture, transport you to a time of extravagance and artistic brilliance. Each haveli tells a story of a prosperous merchant family's rise to prominence and their enduring legacy in the region.

Exploring Shekhawati is akin to stepping back in time, where the walls themselves narrate tales of valour, romance and the zest for life. Havelis are not just architectural wonders; they are living testimonies to the craftsmanship and opulence of a bygone era.

5. Skyscrapers: Reaching New Heights

Our journey reaches its zenith in India's megacities, where skyscrapers pierce the skyline and redefine urban living. These towering structures, often housing luxury apartments and commercial spaces, represent the aspirations and economic prowess of modern India.

Mumbai's Worli Sea Face offers a breathtaking view of the city's skyscrapers. Structures like the Palais Royale stand as engineering marvels, redefining luxury living with amenities such as private swimming pools and helipads. These skyscrapers symbolise the convergence of technology and opulence, where the boundaries of what's possible in real estate are continually pushed.

The skyscrapers in India's megacities are not just architectural marvels; they are statements of ambition and progress. They are beacons of India's growing stature on the global stage, attracting investors and residents from around the world.

6. The Intersection of Tradition and Modernity

What makes India's housing landscape truly captivating is the seamless blend of tradition and modernity. As you explore the country, you'll often find a traditional courtyard house in the heart of an urban metropolis or a modern apartment complex nestled in a heritage neighbourhood. This intersection of architectural styles is an indication of India's ability to embrace the past while hurtling toward the future.

For example, Chennai's Mylapore neighbourhood is a microcosm of this fusion. Here, you can find traditional 'Agraharams' – row houses built around a temple – coexisting with modern apartments and commercial spaces. It's a living illustration of how India's housing varieties mirror its dynamic cultural and economic landscape.

The Socio-Economic Landscape of Housing in India:

Housing in India transcends mere architectural expressions, mirroring the vast socioeconomic strata of its population. The spectrum ranges from humble rural dwellings to lavish urban high-rises, each accommodating diverse financial capabilities and lifestyle aspirations.

1. Affordable Housing: A Foundation for Stability

At the foundation of India's housing sector, affordable housing is crucial in fulfilling the elemental need for shelter among millions. Beyond government programs like PMAY, various state-level initiatives and public-private partnerships have increasingly played pivotal roles. These efforts are geared towards developing sustainable housing solutions that are not only cost-effective but also environmentally conscious and community-oriented.

For example, in Bhiwadi, Rajasthan, the rise of affordable housing projects is a response to the burgeoning demand from the local workforce. These developments are tailored to provide practical, economical and pleasant living conditions for individuals and families engaged in the region's industrial sectors. Such projects underscore a nationwide commitment to bridging the housing affordability gap, ensuring that economic growth and urbanisation do not leave the most vulnerable behind.

2. Mid-Range Housing: Balancing Comfort and Budget

Moving up the socioeconomic ladder, mid-range housing options offer a balance between affordability and comfort. These homes are often targeted at the middle-class population, providing modern amenities without straining budgets.

In the thriving city of Pune, mid-range housing projects have mushroomed to accommodate the city's growing IT workforce. These apartments offer a comfortable lifestyle with amenities like swimming pools and gyms, making them an attractive choice for young professionals and families. Mid-range housing represents the aspiration of the emerging middle class for a better quality of life.

3. Luxury Residences: Exclusivity and Extravagance

At the pinnacle of the housing market, luxury residences in India define exclusivity and opulence. These homes are crafted for those who seek the utmost in privacy, personalised services and sophisticated amenities. A prime example is found on Gurgaon's Golf Course Road, which is home to some of the most luxurious residences in the country. Residents here enjoy services ranging from personal concierges to exclusive golf course access, encapsulating a lifestyle of unrivalled luxury and comfort. These homes are not merely places to live; they are carefully curated experiences designed for those who value sophistication and a distinctive lifestyle.

Case Study: The Aralias by DLF

Located in Gurgaon, The Aralias by DLF stands as a beacon of luxury and bespoke living. This premier residential complex is nestled within a lush, green landscape, offering stunning views and an array of world-class amenities including private swimming pools, state-of-the-art fitness centres and dedicated spa facilities. The Aralias caters to a clientele that desires a seamless blend of luxury and convenience, with spacious, beautifully designed interiors and an attention to detail that ensures a premier living experience. This project exemplifies the successful integration of luxury housing within the rapidly developing urban fabric of Gurgaon, highlighting the demand for high-end living solutions in one of India's most dynamic cities.

The Future of Indian Housing:

As India continues its journey toward becoming a global economic powerhouse, the housing landscape is set to evolve further. Sustainability, technology and innovation will shape the homes of tomorrow.

1. Sustainable Living: Eco-Friendly Homes

The shift toward eco-friendly and sustainable housing is gaining momentum. Green buildings, equipped with energy-efficient systems and renewable energy sources, are becoming increasingly popular. These homes not only reduce environmental impact but also lower utility costs for residents.

In Bengaluru, several residential projects are incorporating green building principles. These developments harness rainwater harvesting, solar power and waste management systems, setting the stage for a more sustainable future. Sustainable living is not just an option; it's a necessity in an era when environmental responsibility is paramount.

2. Smart Homes: Technology-Driven Living

The integration of technology into homes is revolutionising the way we live. Smart homes, equipped with automation systems, security features and digital connectivity, offer convenience and security like never before.

Gurugram's Cyber City is at the forefront of the smart home revolution. Apartments and villas in this tech hub come with cutting-edge home automation systems that allow residents to control everything from lighting to security through their smartphones. Smart homes represent the future of convenience and efficiency.

3. Embracing the Diversity of India's Housing

India's housing landscape is an intricate web woven from the threads of tradition, innovation and aspiration. It's a journey that takes you from the simplicity of rural life to the heights of urban luxury. India can embrace its past while boldly stepping into the future.

As you navigate the pages of 'Kagaz & Kabza', remember that India's real estate story is not just about properties; it's about people and their dreams. It's about the millions of families who find comfort in modest homes and the few who live in opulent penthouses. It's about the architects and developers who shape the skylines and the policymakers who envision inclusive housing solutions.

The diversity of India's housing reflects the nation's dynamic spirit, where every structure, regardless of its size or style, contributes to the colourful mosaic of our country. It's an invitation to explore, appreciate and embrace the remarkable housing varieties that define India's real estate ecosystem.

In the next subchapter, we will dive deep into a comprehensive exploration of the Buyer's Roadmap, providing you with a comprehensive guide to purchasing property in India. So, let's continue our journey through the intricacies of India's real estate landscape, one chapter at a time.

2.3. The Buyer's Roadmap: A Comprehensive Guide to Purchasing Property

Welcome to the third subchapter of 'Kagaz & Kabza: Decoding the Indian Real Estate Ecosystem'. In our journey to unravel the complexities of India's real estate ecosystem, we now arrive at a pivotal destination: the Buyer's Roadmap. Whether you are a first-time buyer or a seasoned investor, understanding the intricacies of purchasing property in India is essential. In this comprehensive guide, we will walk you through the steps, considerations and strategies to make informed decisions and navigate the real estate market with confidence.

Step 1: Define Your Objectives and Budget

The journey to property ownership begins with a clear understanding of your objectives. Are you buying a home for your family, seeking an investment opportunity or looking for a vacation retreat? Defining your goals will shape your property search and guide your decision-making process.

The Buyer's Roadmap:
A Comprehensive Guide to Purchasing Property

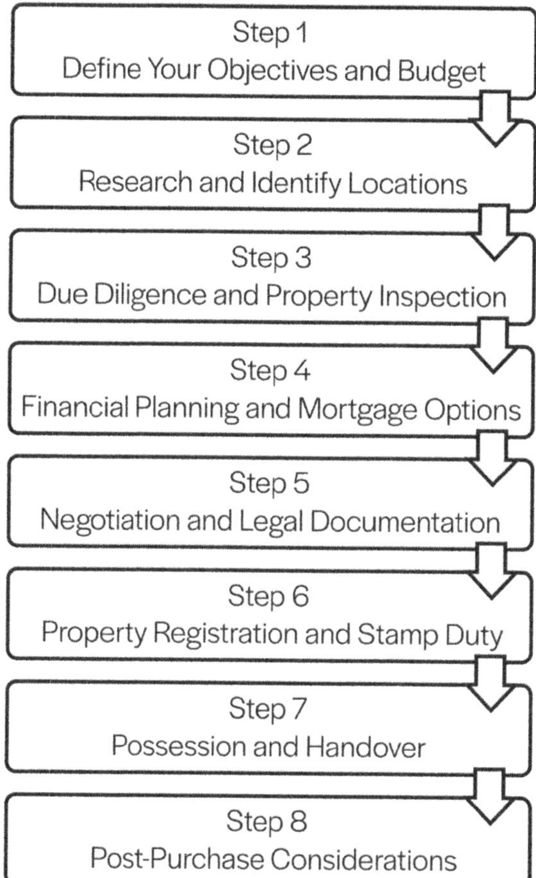

Residential Property:

- **Family Home:** Imagine you're a young couple in Mumbai planning to start a family. Your objective is to purchase a cosy apartment near a good school and healthcare facilities.

- **Investment Property:** Picture yourself as an investor in Bengaluru. Your goal is to generate rental income and capitalise on the city's booming IT sector.

Commercial Property:

- **Commercial Space:** Envision you're an entrepreneur in Delhi aiming to open a retail store. Your objective is to find a bustling commercial area with high foot traffic.

- **Office Space:** Suppose you're an IT company in Hyderabad looking to expand. Your goal is to acquire office space in the city's tech hub to attract top talent.

Once you've defined your objectives, establish a realistic budget. Take into account not only the property's cost but also additional expenses like registration fees, taxes and maintenance. Avoid stretching your budget too thin; it's essential to have financial flexibility to manage unforeseen expenses.

Step 2: Research and Identify Locations

The location of your property plays a significant role in its long-term value and suitability for your needs. India offers a wide range of locations, each with its unique advantages and considerations.

Residential Property:

- **Urban Vs. Suburban:** Consider whether you prefer an urban setting with proximity to city centres or a suburban area with a quieter lifestyle. Urban areas often offer more job opportunities, entertainment options and conveniences, while suburbs provide a peaceful environment.

- **Connectivity:** Assess the connectivity of the location. Access to public transportation, highways and major roads is crucial for daily commuting and long-term convenience.

- **Amenities:** Explore the availability of amenities like schools, hospitals, shopping centres, parks and recreational facilities in the vicinity.

Commercial Property:

- **Target Market:** Identify your target market or clientele. Choose a location that aligns with your business's target audience. For retail businesses, foot traffic and visibility are key. For corporate offices, accessibility and proximity to business hubs matter.

- **Competitive Landscape:** Research the competition in the area. Assess whether the location is already saturated with similar businesses or if there is room for growth and competition.

- **Future Growth:** Analyse the potential for future growth and development in the chosen location. Areas undergoing infrastructure development and urban expansion often present investment opportunities.

Example: Location Selection

Suppose you're considering buying a residential property in Chennai. After researching various neighbourhoods, you discover that the OMR (Old Mahabalipuram Road) area is rapidly developing, with excellent connectivity, schools and healthcare facilities. Additionally, you find that a new IT park is planned nearby, indicating future job opportunities. Based on these findings, you decide that OMR aligns with your objectives of a comfortable family home and potential long-term value appreciation.

Step 3: Due Diligence and Property Inspection

Before committing to a property, conduct thorough due diligence. This step is crucial to ensure that the property meets legal requirements and aligns with your expectations.

Legal Verification:

- **Title Deed:** Verify the property's title deed to ensure clear and marketable ownership. Check for any encumbrances, pending litigation or disputes related to the property.

- **Land Use and Zoning**: Understand the land use and zoning regulations in the area. Ensure that the property's intended use complies with local zoning laws.

- **Approvals and Permits**: Check if the property has obtained the necessary approvals and permits from local authorities. This is particularly important for new construction or redevelopment projects.

Property Inspection:

- **Physical Inspection**: Physically inspect the property to assess its condition, structural integrity and any potential maintenance or renovation requirements.

- **Documentation Review**: Review all property-related documents, including building plans, property tax records and occupancy certificates. Ensure that the property's dimensions and specifications match the documentation.

Example: Due Diligence and Inspection

Imagine you've found a promising residential property in Pune's Wakad area. During due diligence, you discover that the property's title deed is clear and there are no disputes. However, a physical inspection reveals that the roof requires repairs due to water leakage issues. You factor in the repair costs and negotiate with the seller to address the issue before finalising the purchase.

Step 4: Financial Planning and Mortgage Options

Financing your property purchase is a critical aspect of the buying process. Evaluate your financial resources and explore mortgage options if needed.

Financial Assessment:

- **Down Payment:** Determine the amount you can allocate as a down payment. A larger down payment can lead to lower monthly mortgage payments.

- **Credit Score:** Check your credit score and work on improving it if necessary. A higher credit score can help you secure a mortgage at favourable terms.

- **Monthly Budget:** Create a monthly budget that includes mortgage payments, property taxes, maintenance costs and other related expenses. Ensure that your budget remains manageable.

Mortgage Options:

- **Home Loan:** Research home loan options offered by banks and financial institutions. Compare interest rates, repayment terms and eligibility criteria.

Step 5: Negotiation and Legal Documentation

Once you've identified the property you wish to purchase and secured financing, you can initiate the negotiation process with the seller.

Negotiation:

- **Price Negotiation:** Negotiate the property's price with the seller based on market trends, property condition and your budget. Be prepared to make a competitive offer.

- **Terms and Conditions:** Discuss the terms and conditions of the sale, including the timeline, payment schedule and any included furnishings or fixtures.

Legal Documentation:

- **Sale Agreement:** Draft a sale agreement that outlines the terms of the transaction, including the sale price, payment schedule, possession date and any conditions that must be met.

- **Due Diligence:** Ensure that all due diligence, including legal verification and property inspection, has been completed satisfactorily before signing the agreement.

Example: Negotiation and Sale Agreement pop

Suppose you're negotiating with the seller of a residential property in Jaipur. After thorough discussions, you agree on the sale price, a payment schedule and the possession date. You also specify that the sale is contingent on the successful completion of all legal and structural due diligence. Both parties then sign a sale agreement that incorporates these terms and conditions. This agreement safeguards your interests and ensures that the transaction proceeds smoothly.

Step 6: Property Registration and Stamp Duty

Property registration is a legal requirement in India. It is essential to complete the registration process to establish legal ownership of the property.

Property Registration:

- **Stamp Duty:** Pay the applicable stamp duty, which varies from state to state, based on the property's value. Stamp duty is a substantial expense in property transactions.

- **Registration Office:** Visit the local sub-registrar office to complete the registration process. Both the buyer and seller must be present, along with witnesses.

- **Title Transfer:** During registration, the property's title is transferred from the seller to the buyer. This legalises the ownership transfer.

Example: Property Registration

Upon finalising the purchase of your residential property in Hyderabad, you are required to pay the stamp duty and register the property. You visit the local sub-registrar office, accompanied by the seller and witnesses. The property's title is officially transferred to your name and you receive a registered sale deed as proof of ownership. This step ensures that your ownership rights are legally recognised.

Step 7: Possession and Handover

Once the property is registered in your name, you can take possession. This step marks the culmination of your property purchase journey.

Property Handover:

- **Physical Possession:** Ensure that the seller hands over physical possession of the property on the agreed-upon possession date.

- **Documentation:** Collect all property-related documents, including the sale deed, occupancy certificate and property tax records.

- **Utilities and Services:** Transfer utility connections, such as water and electricity, to your name. Ensure that all services are active and functional.

Example: Property Possession

After completing the property registration for your newly purchased residential apartment in Mumbai, the seller officially hands over the keys to the unit on the agreed possession date. You receive all relevant documents, including the sale deed and occupancy certificate. You promptly transfer the utility connections to your name to ensure a seamless transition to your new home.

Step 8: Post-Purchase Considerations (PPC) & Property Management

Your responsibilities as a property owner extend beyond the purchase. Be prepared to address ongoing requirements and responsibilities.

Maintenance and Upkeep:

- **Regular Maintenance:** Plan for regular maintenance and upkeep of the property to ensure its longevity and value retention.

- **Property Tax:** Stay updated on property tax payments to avoid penalties and legal issues.

- **Insurance:** Consider property insurance to protect against unforeseen events like natural disasters or accidents.

Property Management:

- **Tenant Management:** If renting out the property, manage tenant relationships, including lease agreements, rent collection and addressing tenant concerns.

- **Financial Management:** Keep accurate financial records, manage budgets for maintenance and repairs and ensure timely payment of all bills and dues.

- **Legal Compliance:** Stay informed about and comply with all relevant local and state property regulations and laws.

- **Professional Services:** Consider hiring a property management company or a professional real estate advisor for handling maintenance, tenant relations and financial management, especially for properties located far from your residence.

Example: Property Management

As the owner of a residential villa in Goa, you understand the importance of regular maintenance to preserve the property's value. You establish a maintenance schedule that includes periodic inspections, repairs and landscaping. Additionally, you stay vigilant about property tax payments to avoid any legal complications. To manage your property effectively, you decide to hire a property management company that handles tenant relationships, ensures timely rent collection and keeps up with legal compliance. By proactively addressing maintenance, financial and management responsibilities, you ensure the long-term well-being and profitability of your property.

Conclusion:

The Buyer's Roadmap serves as your compass in the intricate world of Indian real estate. It empowers you to make informed decisions, avoid common pitfalls and embark on your property ownership journey with confidence. Whether you're seeking a family home, an investment property or a commercial space, the principles of due diligence, financial planning and legal compliance remain constant.

As you navigate the real estate landscape, remember that each property has its unique story and your role as a buyer is to find the one that aligns with your aspirations. Whether it's the charm of a traditional village dwelling, the elegance of a colonial bungalow, the convenience of an urban apartment, the grandeur of a haveli or the heights of a skyscraper, India's diverse housing varieties offer something for every discerning buyer.

In the next subchapter, we will explore the strategies and considerations for sellers in the Indian real estate market. Understanding the Seller's Strategies is crucial not only for those looking to sell but also for buyers seeking opportunities in this dynamic ecosystem.

2.4. Investment Insights: Trends, Opportunities and Pitfalls

Your budget is the cornerstone of your real estate aspirations; build it wisely.

In the dynamic landscape of Indian real estate, investors play a pivotal role in shaping market trends and driving economic growth. Whether you are a seasoned real estate investor or someone considering real estate as an investment avenue, it's essential to stay informed about the latest trends, opportunities and potential pitfalls in the Indian market.

Current Trends in Real Estate Investment:

1. Residential Segment Dominance:

The residential real estate segment continues to dominate the Indian market. This dominance is driven by increased demand for affordable and mid-segment housing. Emerging trends within this segment include the growing emphasis on eco-friendly and sustainable housing solutions.

Affordable Housing: One of the most significant trends in residential real estate is the focus on affordable housing which has spurred the development of affordable housing projects across the country. These initiatives aim to provide housing to millions of Indians, making it an attractive investment opportunity for both developers and individual investors.

The affordable housing segment has witnessed significant growth in recent years, driven by factors such as government incentives, urbanisation and the rising aspirations of the middle-class population. Investors are increasingly targeting this segment due to its potential for steady returns.

Sustainable and Eco-Friendly Housing: With environmental consciousness on the rise, there's a growing demand for sustainable and eco-friendly housing options. Developers are incorporating features like rainwater harvesting, solar panels and green building materials into their projects. Investors who prioritise sustainability can benefit from the increasing popularity of such properties.

Sustainable and eco-friendly housing aligns with both environmental goals and long-term cost savings. This trend is expected to gain momentum as awareness about environmental issues grows among buyers and investors alike.

2. Co-Living and Co-Working:

India's urbanisation and evolving work patterns have fueled the growth of the co-living and co-working sectors. These trends present new investment opportunities as they cater to the needs of young professionals, students, startups and freelancers.

Co-Living: Co-living spaces offer shared accommodations with amenities, appealing to millennials and professionals who prioritise affordability and community living. These spaces typically include furnished accommodations with shared facilities such as kitchens, common areas and recreational spaces.

Investment Opportunities: Investors can explore opportunities in the co-living sector by partnering with co-living operators or developing their own co-living properties.

The popularity of co-living spaces in urban areas with high housing costs provides a lucrative opportunity for investors.

Example: In cities like Mumbai and Bangalore, co-living spaces have gained traction due to their convenience and cost-effectiveness, making them an attractive option for young professionals seeking community-oriented living arrangements.

Co-Working: The demand for flexible office solutions has led to significant expansion in the co-working sector. Co-working spaces provide startups and freelancers with cost-effective and adaptable office environments.

Investment Opportunities: Investors can consider investing in co-working companies or acquiring commercial properties suitable for co-working setups.

The co-working trend offers opportunities to invest in providers or properties in prime office locations, transforming traditional business operations.

Example: Major cities like Delhi and Hyderabad have witnessed a surge in co-working spaces, driven by the need for flexible, scalable office solutions for businesses of all sizes.

3. Smart Cities and Infrastructure:

The Indian government's ambitious smart city projects and infrastructure development initiatives have garnered attention from investors. Investments in smart cities aim to create technologically advanced urban centres with enhanced livability and connectivity.

This development offers investment opportunities in both residential and commercial real estate.

Residential Opportunities: Smart cities often prioritise sustainable and efficient living, making them attractive for residential real estate investments. The integration of technology, efficient transportation systems and modern amenities can drive property value appreciation.

Investors looking to capitalise on the smart city trend can consider residential properties in these emerging urban centres. The development of smart cities often includes the creation of housing complexes, apartments and gated communities designed to meet modern lifestyle demands.

Commercial Potential: The development of smart cities includes the creation of business districts and commercial hubs. Investors can explore opportunities in office spaces, retail centres and logistics facilities within these emerging urban centres.

Investing in commercial properties in smart cities can provide exposure to growing business districts and retail markets. These areas are expected to attract companies and retailers seeking to establish a presence in technologically advanced urban centres.

4. Technology Integration:

Real estate technology, often referred to as PropTech, is revolutionising the industry. Investors are keen on PropTech-driven innovations, which enhance the convenience and transparency of property transactions.

Online Property Transactions: Online platforms and real estate websites have simplified property transactions. Investors can explore opportunities in PropTech companies that offer digital property listing and transaction services.

The integration of technology in property transactions has streamlined the buying and selling process. Investors can participate in the growth of PropTech companies by considering investments or partnerships in this sector.

Virtual Property Tours: Virtual reality (VR) and augmented reality (AR) are being used to provide immersive property tours. This technology can improve the marketing and showcasing of properties, attracting potential buyers and tenants.

Blockchain-Based Transactions: Blockchain technology is gaining traction in property transactions due to its security and transparency features. Investors interested in blockchain can explore startups and companies working on real estate blockchain solutions.

Blockchain has the potential to revolutionise property transactions by providing a secure and transparent ledger for recording ownership and transactions. Investors can consider blockchain-related projects as part of their investment portfolio.

Investment Opportunities: While understanding the current trends is crucial, identifying investment opportunities is equally important for investors looking to enter or expand their presence in the Indian real estate market. Here are some investment opportunities to consider:

1. Tier 2 and Tier 3 Cities:

While major metropolitan areas like Mumbai, Delhi and Bengaluru continue to attract investors, emerging Tier 2 and Tier 3 cities offer untapped potential. These cities often have lower entry barriers and can provide attractive returns on investment.

Factors to Consider:

Infrastructure Development: Look for cities with ongoing or planned infrastructure development projects. Improved connectivity and amenities can drive property demand.

Economic Growth: Assess the economic growth prospects of the city. Factors like industrial development, job opportunities and GDP growth can indicate investment potential.

Affordability: Consider the affordability of properties in these cities. Lower property prices compared to major metros can attract buyers and renters.

Investing in Tier 2 and Tier 3 cities requires thorough market research and an understanding of local dynamics. These cities may offer higher rental yields and the potential for property value appreciation.

2. Affordable Housing:

Affordable housing initiatives by the government, such as Pradhan Mantri Awas Yojana (PMAY), present investment opportunities. These initiatives aim to make homeownership accessible to a broader population, especially for first-time homebuyers.

Investment Strategies:

Partnerships: Collaborate with developers specialising in affordable housing projects. Partnering with them can provide access to a steady stream of potential buyers.

Rental Income: Consider investing in affordable rental properties. These properties can generate consistent rental income, making them attractive for long-term investors.

Affordable housing projects often come with government incentives and subsidies, making them financially viable for both developers and investors. Investors can participate in this segment to contribute to the government's housing goals while earning returns.

3. Commercial Real Estate:

The commercial real estate sector in India is witnessing growth, with increasing demand for office spaces, retail centres and warehousing facilities. Investments in commercial properties offer rental income potential and can diversify an investment portfolio.

Segments to Explore:

Office Spaces: Consider investing in commercial office spaces in business districts and IT hubs. Leasing to established companies or startups can provide stable rental income.

Retail Centers: Retail properties in prime locations with high footfall can be lucrative. Explore investments in shopping malls or high-street retail spaces.

Warehousing and Logistics: With the growth of e-commerce, there's a rising demand for warehousing and logistics properties. These properties can offer long-term rental contracts with e-commerce companies.

Commercial real estate investments can provide steady rental income and the potential for capital appreciation. Investors can diversify their portfolios by allocating funds to different commercial property segments.

Potential Pitfalls to Watch Out For:

1. Regulatory Changes:

The Indian real estate market is subject to regulatory changes and policy updates, making it crucial for investors to stay vigilant and adaptable. These changes can range from modifications in land acquisition laws and alterations in taxation policies to amendments in property registration rules. Any of these changes can have a significant impact on the feasibility and profitability of real estate investments.

Mitigation:

Legal and Regulatory Experts: Investors should have a team of legal and regulatory experts to assess the implications of new regulations on their investments. These professionals can provide insights into how specific regulatory changes may affect property transactions, ownership and taxation.

Industry Associations: Active participation in industry associations and forums can provide valuable information on upcoming regulatory changes. These networks often have access to policymakers and advocate for the interests of real estate investors.

2. Market Volatility:

Real estate markets are not immune to macroeconomic factors and market fluctuations. Economic instability, currency devaluation or sudden economic downturns can all impact property prices and demand. Market volatility can pose a risk to investors, especially those who rely on short-term investments or have concentrated portfolios.

Mitigation:

Diversification: Diversifying a real estate portfolio is a proven strategy to mitigate market volatility. Investors can consider a mix of asset classes, including residential, commercial and industrial properties, as well as different geographic locations. This diversification helps spread risk and reduce exposure to a single market's ups and downs.

Long-Term Investments: A long-term investment approach can help investors weather short-term market fluctuations. Real estate values tend to appreciate over time and long-term investors can benefit from rental income and capital appreciation.

3. Due Diligence:

Inadequate due diligence can lead to unforeseen issues with properties, titles or legal compliance. Insufficient research can result in financial losses and legal implications for investors. Due diligence is a critical step that involves thoroughly assessing the property's condition, verifying titles and ensuring all legal requirements are met.

Mitigation:

Professional Expertise: Engage professionals such as property lawyers, surveyors and title search experts to conduct due diligence on prospective properties. Property lawyers can review legal documents, contracts and agreements, while surveyors can assess the physical condition of the property. Title search experts can verify ownership history and check for any encumbrances or disputes related to the property.

Property Inspection: A comprehensive property inspection is essential to identify any structural or maintenance issues. Investors should hire qualified inspectors who can provide detailed reports on the property's condition, including necessary repairs or renovations.

4. Overleveraging:

Overleveraging occurs when investors borrow excessively to finance their real estate investments, resulting in a high loan-to-value (LTV) ratio. While leverage can amplify returns in favourable market conditions, it also exposes investors to significant financial risks, especially if market conditions change unfavourably. Overleveraging can lead to difficulties in servicing loans and even property foreclosure.

Mitigation:

Healthy LTV Ratio: Maintaining a healthy LTV ratio is essential. Investors should ensure that they have sufficient equity in their properties to withstand market fluctuations and loan repayment obligations. Avoiding an excessively high LTV ratio provides a buffer against financial stress.

Contingency Planning: Investors should have a contingency plan in place to address adverse financial situations. This may include setting aside reserves for loan servicing, having access to emergency funds or exploring refinancing options if interest rates rise significantly.

In conclusion, while real estate investment in India offers a spectrum of opportunities, it also comes with its share of potential pitfalls. Mitigating these risks through thorough due diligence, staying informed about regulatory changes and adopting a prudent investment approach is crucial. Investors should align their investment strategies with their financial goals and risk tolerance to navigate the Indian real estate market successfully. With the right approach and risk management, real estate can indeed be a rewarding and lucrative investment avenue in India.

In the next subchapter, we will explore the ongoing digital transformation of the real estate sector and its impact on property transactions, convenience and transparency.

2.5. Technological Transformation: The Digitalisation of Real Estate

"Your property journey is your own;
let knowledge be your guiding star."

In an era characterised by rapid technological advancements, the Indian real estate sector has undergone a profound evolution. The integration of technology, commonly referred to as PropTech (Property Technology), has ushered in a wave of digital transformation, fundamentally reshaping the way real estate functions in India. This subchapter explores the multifaceted aspects of how technology is revolutionising the Indian real estate landscape, making it more convenient, transparent and efficient for all stakeholders involved.

PropTech: Revolutionising Real Estate

A Comprehensive Look at PropTech: PropTech is a vast and dynamic field that encompasses a wide array of innovations and digital tools aimed at streamlining and enhancing various facets of the real estate industry. The primary objective of PropTech is to harness emerging technologies such as Artificial Intelligence (AI), Big Data, Augmented Reality (AR) and the Internet of Things (IoT) to drive innovation within the sector. This transformation extends to multiple aspects of real estate, including property search, transactions, property management and sustainability practices.

PropTech is not just a technological trend; it represents a paradigm shift in how the real estate industry operates. Let's explore into how various dimensions of PropTech are reshaping real estate in India:

Transforming Property Search and Discovery:

1. Online Property Portals:

Online property portals have emerged as game-changers in the realm of property search in India. These platforms boast extensive databases of properties, empowering users to refine their property searches based on specific criteria such as location, price range, property type and desired amenities.

Key Benefits of Online Property Portals:

Convenience: Prospective buyers and renters can explore a vast array of properties from the comfort of their homes, eliminating the initial necessity for physical property visits.

Comprehensive Information: Property listings on these portals provide an abundance of information, including detailed property descriptions, high-quality images and increasingly, immersive virtual tours or 360-degree views, offering potential buyers a comprehensive preview of the property.

Time Efficiency: Property seekers can efficiently save time by shortlisting properties that closely align with their preferences before scheduling physical visits.

2. Virtual Reality (VR) and Augmented Reality (AR):

The introduction of Virtual Reality (VR) and Augmented Reality (AR) technologies has ushered in a new era of immersive property viewing experiences in India. Utilising VR headsets or AR-enabled mobile applications, users can take on virtual tours of properties, gaining a realistic and interactive sense of the space before considering physical visits.

Key Benefits of VR and AR in Property Viewing:

Realistic Previews: VR and AR technologies empower potential buyers and tenants to explore properties as if they were physically present, significantly reducing the necessity for multiple site visits.

Enhanced Decision-Making: These immersive technologies allow users to visualise how they can furnish and personalise a space, facilitating more informed and confident decision-making.

Global Accessibility: Overseas investors and buyers can now remotely tour properties, making cross-border investments in the Indian real estate market more accessible and well-informed.

Revolutionising Transactions and Transactions:

1. Online Property Transactions:

Digitalisation has streamlined property transactions in India, ushering in a new era of efficiency and transparency. Online platforms now offer end-to-end solutions, covering every step of the property transaction process, from property listing to document verification and electronic signatures.

Key Benefits of Online Property Transactions:

Efficiency: Transactions that once required physical presence and extensive paperwork can now be efficiently completed online, substantially reducing administrative complexities and time.

Transparency: Digital platforms frequently provide real-time updates on transaction progress, fostering transparency and trust among buyers, sellers and intermediaries.

Security: Advanced encryption and robust security protocols safeguard sensitive transaction data, reducing the risk of fraud and ensuring the integrity of property transactions.

2. Blockchain Technology:

Blockchain technology has garnered substantial attention within the Indian real estate sector due to its unparalleled security and transparency features. This technology offers a tamper-proof, decentralised ledger for recording property ownership and transactions, significantly reducing the risk of fraud, disputes and inefficient record-keeping practices.

Key Benefits of Blockchain in Real Estate Transactions:

Title Verification: Blockchain simplifies the often intricate and time-consuming title verification process, minimising the time and costs associated with title searches.

Reduced Dependence on Intermediaries: Smart contracts, powered by blockchain technology, can automate payment and contract execution, diminishing the need for intermediaries and associated fees.

Trust and Transparency: All parties involved in a real estate transaction can access a secure and transparent record of all steps in the process, thereby minimising disputes and fraudulent activities.

Enhancing Property Management and Operations:

1. Property Management Software:

Property Management Software (PMS) solutions have become indispensable tools for property owners and managers in India, revolutionising the way they handle operations. These sophisticated platforms offer a range of features and benefits that enhance efficiency, tenant engagement and data-driven decision-making.

Key Benefits of Property Management Software:

Streamlined Efficiency: PMS automates routine tasks, from rent collection to maintenance scheduling, significantly reducing manual workloads. This not only minimises the chance of errors but also frees up valuable time for property managers to focus on strategic aspects of property management.

Enhanced Tenant Engagement: Tenants can utilise these platforms to report maintenance issues promptly, pay rent online and communicate with property managers. This enhanced communication fosters positive tenant relationships, resulting in higher satisfaction and retention rates.

Data-Driven Insights: PMS generates a wealth of data and analytics, providing property owners with valuable insights into their properties' performance. These insights can be used to optimise operations, predict maintenance needs and improve overall tenant satisfaction.

2. Internet of Things (IoT):

The Internet of Things (IoT) is rapidly gaining ground in the Indian real estate sector, transforming the way properties are managed and operated. IoT devices, encompassing smart home systems, sensors and devices, enable property owners and managers to monitor and control various aspects of their properties with unprecedented efficiency.

Key Benefits of IoT in Property Management:

Energy Efficiency: IoT devices optimise energy consumption, leading to reduced utility costs for both residential and commercial properties. For instance, smart thermostats can intelligently control heating and cooling systems, ensuring that energy is used only when necessary.

Enhanced Security: Smart security systems equipped with IoT technology offer real-time monitoring and alerts. Property owners and managers can receive notifications about unauthorised access or security breaches, enhancing property safety and reducing vulnerabilities.

Remote Management: Property owners and managers can remotely monitor and control property systems, even from remote locations. This capability improves operational efficiency by allowing quick responses to maintenance needs or security concerns.

3. Sustainability and Green Real Estate:

Sustainability has emerged as a significant concern within the Indian real estate sector, driven by environmental consciousness, regulatory requirements and cost savings. Technological advancements play a pivotal role in promoting eco-friendly practices and the development of green buildings.

Energy-Efficient Technologies:

Incorporating energy-efficient technologies into real estate properties is more than just a trend; it's a necessity. Technologies such as solar panels, smart HVAC systems and energy-efficient lighting are making significant strides in reducing a property's carbon footprint and operating costs.

Key Benefits of Energy-Efficient Technologies:

Cost Savings: Energy-efficient technologies can lead to substantial long-term cost savings on utility bills. Properties equipped with solar panels, for example, can generate their electricity, reducing reliance on conventional grid power.

Environmental Impact: Reduced energy consumption directly contributes to environmental sustainability. Additionally, it aligns with regulatory requirements aimed at curbing carbon emissions and conserving resources.

4. Smart Building Management:

Smart building management systems, driven by IoT and data analytics, represent a holistic approach to optimising resource utilisation, improving occupant comfort and reducing energy waste in properties.

Key Benefits of Smart Building Management:

Resource Optimisation: These systems continuously monitor and control lighting, heating, cooling and other systems to minimise resource wastage. For instance, smart lighting systems adjust brightness based on natural light, reducing unnecessary energy consumption.

Enhanced Comfort: Smart systems can adapt to occupant preferences, ensuring a comfortable environment while conserving resources. Individual temperature control, for example, allows tenants to customise their heating and cooling settings.

Conclusion:

The digitalisation of real estate in India represents a transformative wave that is reshaping how properties are bought, sold, managed and developed. PropTech innovations have not only made property search and discovery more accessible and convenient but have also made transactions more efficient and transparent and property management more streamlined and data-driven.

As the sector continues to embrace technological advancements, stakeholders must adapt, ensuring data security, promoting adoption and preparing for future trends. The future of Indian real estate is undoubtedly tech-enabled, offering opportunities for investors, developers and property seekers to benefit from a more connected and efficient real estate ecosystem.

In the next subchapter, we will explore the intricate dynamics of market fluctuations, understanding price fluctuations and demand trends, which are essential aspects for anyone looking to navigate the Indian real estate market effectively.

-75-

2.6. Market Dynamics: Understanding Price Fluctuations and Demand Trends

"A well-researched decision is the foundation of a successful property investment."

The Indian real estate market is a dynamic ecosystem influenced by a multitude of factors that drive property prices and demand. Navigating this complex landscape requires a comprehensive understanding of the market dynamics that shape the industry. In this subchapter, we will deep dive into the intricate web of forces that exert their influence on the Indian real estate market, providing readers with valuable insights into its functioning.

Economic Factors:

Gross Domestic Product (GDP): The Pulse of the Market

The performance of the Indian economy is an unequivocal driver of the real estate market's health. As the GDP grows, so does the purchasing power of individuals and businesses. This often stimulates increased demand for both residential and commercial real estate.

Example: During the economic boom of the mid-2000s, India experienced rapid GDP growth, which led to a surge in demand for commercial office spaces in major cities like Bengaluru and Hyderabad.

Interest Rates: The Cost of Borrowing

The lending rates set by the central bank have a significant influence on the cost of borrowing for real estate purchases. When interest rates are low, it becomes more affordable for individuals and businesses to invest in properties, thus increasing demand.

Example: In 2020, the Reserve Bank of India (RBI) reduced interest rates to stimulate economic growth during the COVID-19 pandemic. This move led to a boost in home loan applications and increased demand for housing.

Inflation: The Silent Eroder

Inflation, the persistent rise in prices, erodes the purchasing power of individuals over time. High inflation can discourage real estate investments as it diminishes the value of money, while moderate inflation can be conducive to the market.

Example: Inflation rates, while relatively stable in recent years, have influenced investment decisions. Investors have turned to real estate as a hedge against inflation, seeking to preserve their wealth.

Employment Levels: The Housing Equation

The availability of jobs and employment opportunities in a region plays a pivotal role in determining residential real estate demand. Thriving job markets tend to attract more residents, subsequently increasing the demand for housing.

Example: The growth of the information technology sector in cities like Pune and Chennai has led to an influx of IT professionals, spurring demand for residential properties in these areas.

Demographic Trends:

Urbanisation: The Shift to Cities

India's ongoing urbanisation trend is a formidable driver of real estate demand. As more people migrate from rural areas to cities in pursuit of better opportunities, there is a surge in demand for urban housing and commercial spaces.

Example: The Mumbai Metropolitan Region (MMR) has witnessed rapid urbanisation, with suburban areas like Thane and Navi Mumbai becoming attractive residential destinations due to their proximity to employment hubs.

Millennials and Generation Z: Changing Preferences

Younger generations, including millennials and Generation Z, have distinctive preferences when it comes to real estate. They often prioritise locations with easy access to amenities, public transportation and technology.

Example: Co-living spaces have gained popularity in cities like Bengaluru and Gurugram, catering to the preferences of young professionals seeking convenient and community-oriented housing solutions.

Nuclear Families: Smaller Households

Changing family structures, with more nuclear families and dual-income households, drive demand for smaller, more affordable homes and apartments.

Example: The demand for compact 2BHK and 3BHK apartments has surged in cities like Pune, catering to nuclear families seeking budget-friendly housing.

Regulatory and Policy Factors:

Real Estate Regulation and Development Act (RERA): The Game Changer

The implementation of RERA has been a game-changer in the Indian real estate sector. It has increased transparency and accountability, thereby boosting consumer trust in the market.

Example: RERA has led to developers becoming more accountable for project delays and deviations from promised specifications, ensuring that buyers receive what was promised.

Goods and Services Tax (GST): The Taxation Overhaul

The introduction of GST replaced multiple taxes with a unified taxation system. This has streamlined tax compliance for real estate transactions, impacting both buyers and sellers.

Example: Under the GST regime, property buyers no longer have to navigate a complex web of taxes, making it easier to calculate and understand their tax liabilities.

Land Acquisition Laws: Impact on Development

Changes in land acquisition laws can significantly impact real estate projects by affecting land availability, project timelines and overall feasibility.

Example: The implementation of new land acquisition laws in states like Haryana has led to increased transparency and expedited land acquisition processes, benefiting developers.

Supply and Demand Dynamics:

Housing Shortages: Bridging the Gap

India grapples with a significant shortage of affordable housing, especially in burgeoning urban centres. This presents a substantial opportunity for developers and investors to fill the void by focusing on affordable housing developments. Innovative financing options and schemes, such as housing bonds or subsidies for low-income home buyers, are increasingly being leveraged to promote affordable housing. Additionally, state and local governments are collaborating with private developers to streamline land acquisition and expedite regulatory processes, making it easier and more attractive to invest in affordable housing projects.

Example: Initiatives like tax incentives for developers who build affordable units and the facilitation of community housing projects through non-profit partnerships reflect a multi-faceted approach to tackling the housing crisis. These strategies aim to not only increase the availability of affordable homes but also make homeownership more achievable for the economically disadvantaged segments of the population.

Excess Inventory: The Balancing Act

In some cases, oversupply can lead to downward pressure on property prices. Understanding local inventory levels is crucial for making informed investment decisions.

Example: The oversupply of luxury apartments in some areas of Gurugram led to price corrections, making high-end properties more affordable for buyers.

Location and Accessibility: The Geography of Demand

Proximity to transportation hubs, educational institutions, healthcare facilities and commercial centres significantly influences demand. Properties in well-connected areas tend to command higher prices.

Example: Properties located near metro stations in Delhi-NCR have seen increased demand due to the convenience they offer for daily commuting.

Market Sentiment:

Investor Sentiment: Speculative Influences

Real estate markets are often influenced by investor sentiment. Positive sentiment can lead to speculative buying, potentially driving up prices. Conversely, negative sentiment can result in a downturn.

Example: Positive announcements regarding infrastructure projects can boost investor sentiment, leading to increased investments in the affected regions.

Consumer Confidence: The Trust Factor

The confidence of homebuyers and investors in the market is a key driver of demand. Factors such as political stability and economic outlook can influence consumer confidence.

Example: Periods of political stability and transparent governance have often resulted in increased consumer confidence and higher real estate investments.

Case Study: Mumbai's Real Estate Market

To illustrate the impact of these market dynamics, let's take a closer look at the real estate market in Mumbai, one of India's largest and most dynamic cities.

Economic Factors: Mumbai's status as India's financial capital means it is highly influenced by economic factors. Fluctuations in GDP growth, interest rates and inflation directly impact property prices. During the economic boom of the mid-2000s, India experienced rapid GDP growth, which led to a surge in demand for commercial office spaces in major cities like Bengaluru and Hyderabad.

Demographic Trends: Mumbai's population is diverse, with a mix of millennials, professionals and families. Developers have adapted to these demographics by offering a wide range of housing options, from luxury apartments to compact, affordable homes. Areas with good connectivity and proximity to employment hubs are especially sought after.

Regulatory and Policy Factors: The implementation of RERA has significantly improved transparency and consumer protection in Mumbai's real estate market. Homebuyers are now more confident about investing in the city.

Supply and Demand Dynamics: Mumbai faces a persistent shortage of affordable housing, leading to high demand for budget-friendly options. However, some upscale areas in South Mumbai have seen an oversupply of luxury apartments, which has affected prices in those regions.

Market Sentiment: Mumbai's real estate market is known for its investor-driven sentiment. Positive news, such as infrastructure developments or new business hubs, can trigger increased investments, while negative events, like policy uncertainties or economic slowdowns, can lead to market corrections.

Understanding the dynamics of Mumbai's real estate market provides valuable insights into how local and global factors interact to shape property prices and demand. Similar dynamics play out in various Indian cities, albeit with some regional variations.

Strategies for Navigating Market Dynamics:

Given the complex and ever-changing nature of real estate market dynamics, adopting sound strategies is essential for successful navigation:

Market Research: Conduct thorough research on the specific region and segment you're interested in. Analyse economic indicators, demographic trends and regulatory factors to make informed decisions.

Diversification: Diversify your real estate portfolio across different types of properties and locations. This can help mitigate risks associated with market fluctuations.

Long-Term Perspective: Real estate investments often yield better returns over the long term. Short-term fluctuations may occur, but a patient approach can lead to substantial gains.

Local Expertise: Engage with local real estate experts and agents who have a deep understanding of the market. Their insights can be invaluable in making strategic investments.

Risk Management: Assess and mitigate risks associated with market volatility, economic downturns and regulatory changes. Having contingency plans in place is essential.

Stay Informed: Continuously monitor market trends, economic developments and policy changes. Staying informed allows you to adapt your strategies accordingly.

Conclusion:

Understanding the intricate market dynamics of the Indian real estate sector is crucial for anyone looking to buy, sell or invest in properties. Economic factors, demographic trends, regulatory changes and market sentiment all play a role in shaping property prices and demand.

By staying informed, adopting a long-term perspective and diversifying investments, individuals and businesses can successfully navigate the ever-evolving landscape of the Indian real estate market. Mumbai's real estate market serves as an example of how these dynamics can impact a major city and similar principles apply to real estate markets across India.

2.7. Eco-Friendly Investment and Development

The Indian real estate landscape is undergoing a profound transformation, one that aligns with the global shift toward sustainability and environmental consciousness. The concept of eco-friendly investment and development has gained significant traction in recent years, reshaping the real estate sector in India. In this extensive exploration of the topic, we explore deeper into the pivotal role of eco-friendliness in the Indian real estate industry. From green building practices to sustainable technologies and the financial rewards that follow, we will uncover how these initiatives are not only environmentally responsible but also financially lucrative for both investors and developers.

The Green Revolution in Real Estate:

The 'Green Revolution' in Indian real estate represents a paradigm shift toward sustainable and eco-friendly practices. Developers, investors and homebuyers have increasingly recognised the benefits of eco-friendly construction and sustainable development. Let's explore into the key aspects of this transformation:

Green Building Certifications: Setting the Standards

One of the pillars of eco-friendly real estate is the certification of buildings based on their sustainability standards. Certifications like LEED (Leadership in Energy and Environmental Design), IGBC (Indian Green Building Council) and GRIHA (Green Rating for Integrated Habitat Assessment) evaluate and validate environmentally responsible building practices.

Example: The Infosys Limited campus in Mysuru, Karnataka, sets a remarkable example of eco-friendly construction. It has achieved LEED Platinum certification, incorporating energy-efficient design, rainwater harvesting and extensive green landscaping into its infrastructure.

Energy-Efficient Technologies: Reducing Carbon Footprint

Energy efficiency is at the heart of eco-friendly real estate. The integration of energy-efficient technologies, such as solar panels, smart HVAC systems and LED lighting, significantly reduces a property's carbon footprint while simultaneously lowering operational costs.

Example: The Wave Group's Wave City Center in Noida boasts India's largest solar carport, generating renewable energy to power the project's common areas. This not only reduces the project's carbon emissions but also lowers energy costs.

Waste Reduction and Recycling: Sustainable Practices

Sustainable construction practices aim to reduce waste generation and promote recycling. Eco-friendly projects incorporate waste segregation and recycling systems, thereby minimising the environmental impact of construction.

Example: The Godrej Garden City in Ahmedabad has made substantial strides in sustainable waste management practices, diverting a significant portion of construction waste from landfills and promoting recycling.

Image source: medium.com (https://medium.com/@projects
properties13/godrej-garden-city-the-wide-spread-township-
in-the-city-of-ahmedabad-d1e275da4f2e)

Government Initiatives and Incentives:

The Indian government plays a pivotal role in promoting eco-friendly investment and development in the real estate sector. Several initiatives and incentives have been introduced to encourage developers and investors to embrace sustainable practices:

Pradhan Mantri Awas Yojana (PMAY): Affordable and Eco-Friendly Housing

PMAY aims to provide affordable housing for all while encouraging eco-friendly construction. Developers who adopt green building practices are eligible for financial incentives under this scheme. Example: The Shriram Greenfield project in Bengaluru is a PMAY-affiliated development that combines affordability with sustainable features, including rainwater harvesting and energy-efficient lighting.

Goods and Services Tax (GST) Benefits: Reduced Taxation for Green Projects

The government offers GST benefits to projects that adhere to green building norms. Reduced GST rates are applied to eco-friendly construction materials and technologies, making sustainable development financially attractive.

Example: The Mahindra World City in Chennai enjoys GST benefits for green building materials and practices, contributing to cost savings for investors.

Case Study: Mahindra Lifespace's Green Initiatives

To exemplify the profound impact of eco-friendly investment and development, let's take a closer look at Mahindra Lifespace Developers Limited, a leading real estate developer in India.

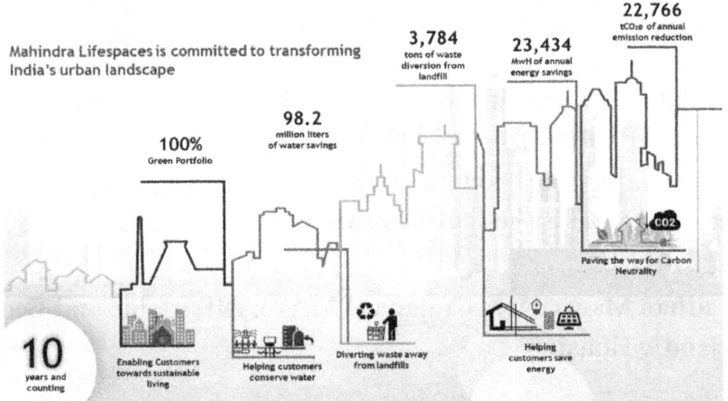

Source: Mahindra Lifespaces (https://www.mahindralifespaces.com/sustainability-core/esg-journey-so-far-roadmap-2025/)

Sustainability as a Core Value: Mahindra Lifespace places sustainability at the core of its projects. The company is committed to achieving carbon neutrality and net-zero waste in its developments.

Water Conservation: In its project Mahindra World City, Chennai, the developer has implemented advanced rainwater harvesting systems to recharge groundwater and reduce dependence on external water sources.

Renewable Energy Integration: Mahindra Lifespace incorporates solar energy solutions into its projects, significantly reducing the carbon footprint of its developments.

Biodiversity and Greenery: The company prioritises green spaces and biodiversity conservation within its projects. It creates urban forests, preserves existing greenery and fosters a harmonious coexistence of nature and urban living.

Green Building Certifications: Many of Mahindra Lifespace's projects, such as Happinest Avadi in Chennai, have achieved prestigious green building certifications, exemplifying their commitment to eco-friendly development.

Eco-Friendly Investment and Financial Returns:

Investors in eco-friendly real estate not only contribute to sustainability but also enjoy financial benefits. Eco-friendly properties often yield attractive returns due to various factors:

- **Reduced Operational Costs:** Energy-efficient technologies and sustainable practices lead to lower operational expenses, enhancing the property's profitability.

- **Higher Rental and Resale Values:** Eco-friendly properties are often in high demand among tenants and buyers who value sustainability, translating into higher rental and resale values.

- **Market Reputation:** Developers with a strong focus on sustainability tend to build a positive reputation, attracting more buyers and investors.

Regulatory Compliance: Eco-friendly projects are more likely to align with changing environmental regulations, reducing the risk of future compliance issues.

Challenges and Considerations:

While the benefits of eco-friendly investment and development are clear, it's essential to acknowledge the challenges and considerations involved:

- **Higher Initial Costs:** Eco-friendly construction can involve higher upfront costs. Developers and investors need to carefully weigh these costs against long-term benefits. **Example:** The use of energy-efficient materials and technologies, while costlier initially, leads to significant savings in energy bills over the property's lifetime.

- **Education and Awareness:** Increasing awareness and education about eco-friendly practices is crucial. Buyers and investors need to understand the long-term advantages of sustainable real estate. **Example:** Developers often conduct awareness campaigns and workshops to educate potential buyers about the environmental and financial benefits of eco-friendly properties.

- **Availability of Green Materials:** The availability of sustainable construction materials can sometimes be limited. Developers must source these materials carefully. **Example:** Sourcing locally produced eco-friendly materials reduces transportation emissions and supports the local economy.

Future Outlook: Sustainable Real Estate

The future of Indian real estate undoubtedly embraces sustainability as a fundamental principle. As the industry evolves, several trends and developments are expected to shape the trajectory of sustainable real estate:

- **Innovations in Building Materials:** The industry will witness the emergence of novel, sustainable building materials that further enhance energy efficiency and reduce environmental impact.

- **Smart Technologies:** Integration of smart technologies, such as IoT (Internet of Things) for energy management and home automation, will become standard in eco-friendly properties.

- **Zero-Energy Buildings:** The concept of zero-energy buildings, where a property generates as much energy as it consumes, will gain prominence.

- **Regulatory Advancements:** Environmental regulations will continue to evolve, encouraging even stricter adherence to eco-friendly construction practices.

- **Community Sustainability:** Developers will focus on creating sustainable communities, not just individual eco-friendly properties, emphasising green spaces, public transportation and community gardens.

Conclusion:

Eco-friendly investment and development have emerged as significant drivers of change in the Indian real estate sector. As sustainability becomes an essential consideration for both developers and investors, the industry is witnessing a transformation toward environmentally responsible practices.

Government initiatives and incentives, along with the commitment of developers like Mahindra Lifespace, are propelling the green revolution in real estate. By adopting green building certifications, embracing energy-efficient technologies and practising sustainable construction, the Indian real estate sector is not only contributing to environmental preservation but also reaping the financial rewards of eco-friendly investments.

"The dynamics of the real estate market are like the tides, constantly influenced by external forces but ever persistent in their rhythm. By grasping the underlying principles and staying attuned to the changes, we can ride these waves with confidence and foresight."

Chapter 3

KAGAZ - The Blueprint for Wise Property Documentation

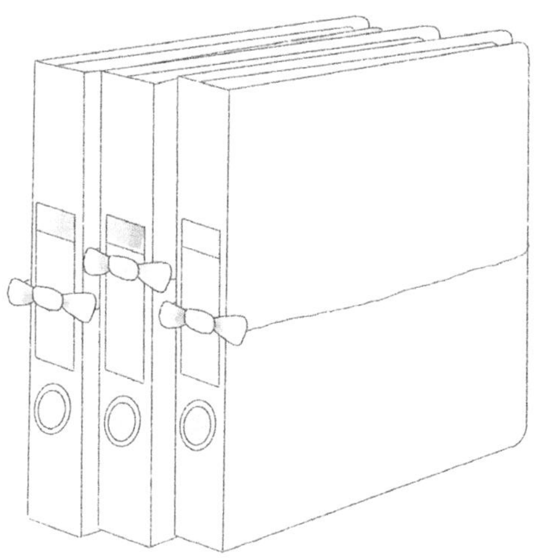

"In the realm of real estate, documentation is the bedrock of security. The meticulous recording of every detail transforms dreams into tangible assets, ensuring that each investment is protected by the armour of legality and clarity."

In this chapter, we explore property transactions, highlighting the crucial role of paperwork or 'KAGAZ' in ensuring secure property documentation. It acts as a strong defence against potential legal challenges that may be hidden in the background.

Why KAGAZ Matters:

KAGAZ, sometimes seen just as paper, is more than that—it holds trust, legality and financial wisdom. It serves as the protector of your real estate dreams and investments, a quiet guardian looking out for your interests. KAGAZ is like a steadfast compass, guiding you safely through the complex terrain of real estate, preventing you from hitting the risky shores of uncertainty.

Imagine every property you've ever called home, every office space where you've meticulously built your ambitions and every piece of land you've viewed as a potential investment opportunity. Each one has a story, a tale meticulously documented, verified and legalised through the indispensable documents of KAGAZ. These documents are not just ordinary pieces of paper; they are the lifeblood of the real estate world, ensuring your property transactions are not only successful but also free from the snares of legal misadventures.

Let me narrate a compelling real-life story that vividly illustrates the profound importance of KAGAZ.

Meet Ramesh and Priya, a young couple in Delhi with a dream of buying their first home—a place to build their future, make lasting memories and find peace from city chaos. As diligent homebuyers, they spent months exploring the real estate market, wanting to find the perfect home. It was a challenging journey, visiting many properties, talking to numerous agents and carefully examining details to ensure their investment was worthwhile.

Their search led them to a fantastic apartment in a new complex that met all their criteria. However, being aware of real estate complexities, they knew appearances could be deceiving. To protect their investment, they conducted due diligence, examining the important documents associated with the property.

Digging into the paperwork, they found crucial information. The builder had obtained all necessary approvals, property titles were clear, confirming land legitimacy, taxes were paid and there were no issues jeopardising ownership. Each document became a puzzle piece, forming a foundation of trust and legality.

Their thorough examination of the paperwork not only gave them confidence but also assured them that their chosen property was legally sound and a secure investment. With hope in their hearts, knowledge in their minds and their paperwork carefully scrutinised, Ramesh and Priya were ready to turn their dream of owning a home into a reality.

As you experience this enlightening journey, consider these pivotal questions:

- Do you possess a comprehensive understanding of the role and significance of each of these documents in a property transaction?

- How can your knowledge of these documents protect you from potential legal and financial pitfalls?

- Have you taken the necessary steps to verify the authenticity and legality of the documents provided by the seller?

The Wisdom of KAGAZ: A Blueprint for Success

K = Knowledge of Necessary Documents

When you explore the importance of paperwork (KAGAZ), think of Knowledge of Necessary Documents, as your protection in the real estate world. These documents aren't just words on paper; they guide you toward your real estate dreams. They carry the stories of past deals, the wisdom from legal disputes and the histories of properties that influence your investments.

In the upcoming chapters, we'll look into each of these documents, uncovering their details, revealing their stories and finding the valuable information within. Armed with this knowledge, you'll not only manage real estate transactions but also succeed in them. So, as you get ready to explore the details of paperwork (KAGAZ), keep in mind: it's not just paper; it's the guide that helps you navigate the complex world of real estate, making sure each step is safe, legal and successful.

In the words of the renowned American author and lecturer, Ralph Waldo Emerson: "Knowledge is the antidote to fear." With KAGAZ as your knowledge guide, fear won't be part of your real estate journey. Instead, you'll follow a path lit by understanding, wisdom and the hope of a better real estate future.

To confidently navigate the real estate world, start by getting familiar with the crucial documents supporting every property transaction. The documents listed below are the strong foundations of secure property dealings:

Title Deed: The Crown Jewel of Ownership

Now, let's explore deeper into the crown jewel of property documents—the Title Deed. This document is not just a piece of paper; it is the embodiment of property ownership rights. It carries with it the legacy of every past owner, each transaction and every legal claim associated with the property.

Consider the heartwarming tale of Mr and Mrs Sharma, a couple who had long dreamt of owning a quaint cottage nestled in the picturesque hills. Their journey led them to the perfect property, a charming abode surrounded by lush greenery, where the air was filled with the melodies of nature. Eager to make this haven their own, they began their journey to seal the deal.

However, their excitement and dreams were soon met with a harsh reality check. During the due diligence process, they discovered that the property's title deed was embroiled in a complex legal dispute, a battle waged in the shadows of the tranquil hills. The Sharmas realised that without a clear and unencumbered title deed, their dreams of a peaceful hillside retreat were in jeopardy.

This poignant story serves as a stark reminder that the Title Deed is not just a mundane piece of paper; it's your unshakable assurance of a legitimate transaction and undisputed ownership. It's the magical key that unlocks the door to your dreams, ensuring that your real estate journey is one of serenity, not sorrow.

Sale Deed: The Transfer of Ownership

Continuing our exploration of essential property documents, we come to the Sale Deed. This legal instrument is the linchpin that facilitates the seamless transfer of property ownership from the seller to the buyer. It is more than a document; it is the indisputable evidence of the transaction itself. Sale Deeds are often executed on a non-judicial stamp paper, with the value varying according to the Stamp Act applicable in your state.

For example, the story of Mr Patel, a shrewd investor with a keen eye for opportunities in the real estate market. His journey led him to a prime commercial property located in a bustling market area—a golden opportunity or so it seemed. The seller, with an air of confidence, assured Mr Patel that the property came with a pristine Sale Deed.

However, Mr Patel, fueled by his meticulous nature, began his due diligence that would prove pivotal. As he scrutinised the Sale Deed, his discerning eye detected discrepancies and subtle irregularities that hinted at a deeper, hidden truth. These red flags prompted him to explore deeper into the property's history.

With the wisdom of a seasoned investor, Mr Patel wisely chose to step away from the deal, thus avoiding a potential quagmire of legal entanglements. This real-life anecdote underscores the paramount importance of scrutinising the Sale Deed to ensure a legitimate, secure transfer of ownership. It teaches us that within the folds of this document lies not just a transaction but the safeguarding of your real estate dreams.

Encumbrance Certificate: A Testament to Freedom

As our journey through essential property documents continues, we come across the Encumbrance Certificate—an often-overlooked but of paramount significance. This document stands as a testament to a property's freedom from legal and financial liabilities, offering you the reassurance that the property is devoid of any pending dues, mortgages or lingering legal disputes.

To truly grasp the importance of the Encumbrance Certificate, let's immerse ourselves in the story of Ms Rao. She is a retiree, on the brink of embracing her golden years, filled with dreams of a peaceful, retired life in a serene residential community. Ms Rao's quest led her to stumble upon a charming villa, nestled within a gated paradise—a place she envisioned as her forever home.

At first glance, the villa seemed like the embodiment of her dreams—a place where she could find solace and happiness in the twilight of her life. But Ms Rao, possessing the wisdom of experience, knew that in the world of real estate, appearances could be deceiving. She enquired, driven by an innate need to protect her future.

During her diligent investigation, she uncovered a revelation that could have easily gone unnoticed by someone less meticulous. The property had an encumbrance due to an unpaid loan by the previous owner. This revelation was a turning point in her real estate journey. The encumbrance, like a hidden serpent, could have struck unexpectedly, leading to financial entanglements that could have shattered her dreams.

Armed with the knowledge gained through the Encumbrance Certificate, Ms Rao made a prudent choice to reconsider her investment. This real-life example illustrates the critical role that this often-overlooked document plays. It is not just a piece of paper; it is a guardian of your hard-earned investment and the protector of your dreams. The Encumbrance Certificate unveils hidden encumbrances, ensuring the safeguarding of your financial security and the preservation of your peace of mind.

Khata Certificate and Extract: The Gateway to Tax Assessment

In many states, a Khata certificate serves as the gateway to property tax assessment—a seemingly mundane document with profound significance. It certifies that the property exists legally and is a crucial prerequisite for property tax assessment. The Khata extract, on the other hand, provides essential details about the property owner and its dimensions.

Let's look at Mr and Mrs Gupta's situation. They are a young couple excited about building their dream home on a piece of inherited land. They have big plans and dreams for their future home—a place where they can build their life together and make lasting memories.

However, as with many journeys, they encountered an unexpected bureaucratic roadblock. Their excitement was met with astonishment when they attempted to secure a Khata certificate from the local municipal authority. To their dismay, they discovered that the land's Khata was still registered in the name of the previous owner's family. This discovery led to a maze of administrative hurdles, creating a daunting obstacle in their path.

Months of tireless effort and persistence were required to finally secure the Khata in their name, a journey filled with frustration and uncertainty. This tale underscores the profound importance of a clear Khata certificate for hassle-free property ownership. It highlights how a seemingly minor oversight can lead to bureaucratic challenges that delay your dream home and test your patience.

In the world of real estate, details matter and each document plays a unique role in ensuring the security of your investment. The Khata certificate and extract may seem like administrative formalities, but they are the keys that unlock the door to legitimate property ownership and hassle-free tax assessment.

Occupancy Certificate: Ensuring Safety and Compliance

In our exploration of essential property documents, the Occupancy Certificate takes centre stage. This document, issued by the local municipal authority, holds immense importance, particularly for properties in multi-story buildings. It serves as a confirmation that the building fully complies with the approved building plan and is deemed fit for occupation. Far from being a mere formality, it is your guarantee of safety and legality within your chosen dwelling.

Let's learn about Mr and Mrs Verma, a newly married couple excited to start their life together in a tall apartment building in a busy city. Their new home meant more than just a place to live; it was the start of their future. They were thrilled about this new chapter until a neighbour mentioned that the building didn't have an Occupancy Certificate.

Concerned about the safety and legality of their residence, the Vermas promptly initiated an investigation. What they uncovered was nothing short of shocking—the builder had not obtained the necessary approvals for the building's occupancy. The absence of the Occupancy Certificate puts not only their dreams but also their safety at risk.

The Vermas' story highlights how crucial the Occupancy Certificate is. It's not just a piece of paper; it safeguards your safety and ensures the integrity of your investment. Without it, the excitement of a new beginning could turn into a risky and uncertain nightmare.

Building Approval Plan: Blueprint for Compliance

In our exploration of vital property documents, let's focus on the Building Approval Plan. This document visually displays the approved plan for the property or building. It declares that the property follows municipal regulations and safety standards, ensuring it complies with the law.

Let's learn the story of Mr Desai, an astute investor with a discerning eye for detail. He had set his sights on purchasing a commercial space to accommodate his expanding business empire. His tireless search led him to what seemed like an ideal property, located in a prime and bustling location. However, Mr Desai's commitment to due diligence went above and beyond the ordinary.

During his investigation, he stumbled upon an unexpected revelation—a revelation that would be the turning point in his property journey. He discovered that the property he intended to purchase had been constructed without the necessary approvals and failed to conform to municipal regulations. At that moment, Mr Desai realised the full gravity of the situation. The absence of the Building Approval Plan was a red flag signalling not just potential legal troubles but also severe financial setbacks.

Mr Desai's prudence and attention to detail not only saved him from potential pitfalls but also underscored the critical importance of the Building Approval Plan. It serves as the blueprint for compliance, ensuring that your investment is grounded in legality and safety. Without it, your dreams of prosperity could be tainted by the shadows of uncertainty.

Power of Attorney: Delegating Authority

In our real estate journey, we now shine a spotlight on the Power of Attorney—a legal document with the potential to empower or, if misused, to betray trust. The Power of Attorney is a valuable instrument, often deployed when a property owner cannot be physically present during a transaction. Yet, this tool comes with a stark duality, holding both convenience and caution within its grasp.

For example, Ms Reddy, a Non-Resident Indian residing abroad, wished to sell her ancestral property in India. The prospect of managing the sale from a distance was daunting and she turned to her cousin, seeing the Power of Attorney as a practical solution. With this document in hand, she entrusted her cousin to act on her behalf. However, what followed was a heartbreaking tale of deception.

Ms Reddy's cousin, driven by ulterior motives, sold the property at a fraction of its true value, pocketing the proceeds for personal gain. This act of betrayal left Ms Reddy not only with substantial financial losses but also with a profound sense of trust. Her experience serves as an unforgettable cautionary tale, underscoring the critical need for careful consideration and scrutiny when granting a Power of Attorney.

The Power of Attorney is like a two-sided tool—it can make things easier or lead to trouble. This document shows us that although it can simplify transactions, it requires careful attention and trust. In real estate, it's a reminder to be cautious and make sure the person you authorise is as trustworthy as you are.

Building Completion Certificate: Assurance of Quality

Our journey through essential property documents now leads us to the Building Completion Certificate—a document that serves as your assurance of quality and safety when investing in an under-construction property. This certificate confirms that the construction has been completed in strict accordance with the approved plan and safety standards, providing you with the confidence that your investment is sound.

Example: Mr Singh was an investor who had acquired a luxurious apartment in a high-end residential complex. The builder had enticed him with promises of unparalleled quality and craftsmanship. However, it was only when Mr Singh received the Building Completion Certificate that he uncovered a disheartening truth. The property had several deviations from the approved plan, compromising not only its safety but also its overall quality.

This situation is a clear reminder of the important role that the Building Completion Certificate plays in ensuring the integrity of your investment. It underscores the importance of scrutinising every document and detail before committing, for it is not just your financial security but also your safety and peace of mind that are at stake.

Property Tax Receipts: Clearing Dues

In the final segment of our exploration into essential property documents, we arrive at the significance of Property Tax Receipts. This seemingly straightforward document holds immense importance—it is imperative to confirm that the seller has cleared all property tax dues up to the date of the transaction. Neglecting this critical aspect can lead to unexpected financial burdens after the purchase.

Example: Mr and Mrs Kapoor were a retired couple eagerly anticipating their new life in their dream home. The joy of moving into their cherished abode was short-lived when they received an unexpected notice shortly after the purchase. It revealed pending property tax payments from the previous owner—an issue they had believed was settled during the transaction.

The Kapoors' experience serves as a cautionary tale, emphasising the need to verify Property Tax Receipts meticulously. It highlights that even in the midst of the excitement of owning a dream home, attention to detail is paramount. Ensuring that all financial aspects are in order can prevent post-purchase surprises and maintain the serenity of your new life journey.

The Sale Deed: Unveiling the Blueprint of Property Ownership

In real estate, the Sale Deed is like the foundation, outlining all the crucial details for transferring property ownership. It contains information about the property, the responsibilities of the parties involved, financial aspects and the specific terms of the exchange. Exploring the Sale Deed reveals its profound significance in the real estate realm.

The Agreement to Sell: Laying the Foundation of Real Estate Dreams

"Every property has a story; it's up to you to read between the lines of documentation."

In real estate, every venture starts with a dream and the Agreement to Sell is at the core of making that dream a reality. This document brings together the seller's aspirations and the buyer's dreams, forming a legally binding commitment. In property transactions, recognising the importance of the Agreement to Sell is like understanding the crucial role of a strong foundation in building a great structure. This explanation sheds light on the document's essence and underscores its vital role in any property transaction's foundation.

The Title Deed and Encumbrance Certificate - Guardians of Clarity:

Digging deeper into the world of property transactions, we encounter a critical duo—the Title Deed and its underestimated document, the Encumbrance Certificate. Together, they create a solid defence against legal claims and financial uncertainties. Acting as diligent guardians, these documents guarantee transparency and legitimacy in property ownership, shielding your investment from possible risks. Join us on this exploration as we explore into the details, accompanied by a real-life case study from Chennai that vividly demonstrates the repercussions of neglecting a comprehensive encumbrance check.

The Power of Legal Expertise:

The Significance of Legal Counsel - Your Guiding Light: Navigating through property paperwork can feel like a dangerous journey. But with the help of a real estate attorney, the way becomes clearer and easier to understand. They shine a light on the complicated parts, making things easier to manage. This section explores deep into the significance of legal consultation, emphasising how it can be your ultimate ally in securing a seamless property transaction. However, to truly grasp its indispensable role, we will soon introduce a compelling real-world case study that vividly illustrates the transformative power of legal expertise.

Diligent Due Diligence - Uncovering Hidden Truths: In the realm of real estate, knowledge is paramount and understanding the true essence of a property is often hidden beneath layers of paperwork. Enter the legal due diligence process—a meticulous examination conducted by a skilled attorney. While we acknowledge its essential role in any property transaction, we believe in the power of real-life stories. Thus, we will soon present a case study that reveals the profound impact of diligent due diligence, unearthing hidden truths that can alter the course of a property deal.

Revealing the Secrets Within KAGAZ:

Property Tax and Utility Bills - Navigating Financial Waters: Beneath the surface of every real estate transaction, there flows a complex river of financial currents—property taxes and utility bills. These often-overlooked elements play a pivotal role in the overall scheme of property dealings. To truly grasp their significance, we will explore deeper into the financial waters, elucidating their importance in ensuring a smooth and hassle-free property transaction. Furthermore, we will introduce a real-life case study to illustrate how a lack of understanding in this area can lead to unforeseen financial burdens.

Builder-Buyer Agreement - The Roadmap for Possession: Your dream property's possession is not merely a matter of fate but a well-defined path paved by the builder-buyer agreement. This vital document holds the keys to when and how you gain access to your cherished property. In this section, we will not only highlight its importance but also navigate through its legal nuances. To add depth to our understanding, a pertinent case study will accompany this discussion, showcasing how the builder-buyer agreement can be your guide to realising the possession of your dream property.

The Essence of Mutation and Property Ownership:

The Significance of Mutation - Cementing Your Ownership: Mutation, often an overlooked aspect of property transactions, is the keystone that officially cements your ownership in the government's eyes. It's not just a bureaucratic formality; it's a critical step in ensuring that your property's title is recognised by the authorities. In this section, we'll explore the profound importance of mutation, emphasising its role as the final stamp of legitimacy on your property ownership journey. To drive this point home, we'll present a compelling case study that vividly showcases the ramifications of overlooking this crucial step.

The Transfer of Ownership - Your Stamp on the Legacy: The process of transferring ownership through mutation can sometimes be shrouded in confusion. In this part of our guide, we will demystify the intricacies of this process, providing readers with a clear and comprehensive understanding. By the end of this section, you will not only appreciate the theoretical aspects but also the practical steps involved in making your mark on the legacy of your property.

Post-Mutation Responsibilities:

Updated Property Tax Records - Securing Your Future: Securing your investment's future isn't just about completing a mutation; it also entails updating property tax records. We'll explore into this crucial post-mutation responsibility, explaining why it's a necessary step. To drive home the importance of this, we'll share a real-world example that highlights the significance of having your property tax records up-to-date.

Legal Validation - Your Shield and Sword: While the concept of legal validation is briefly touched upon, we believe it deserves a closer look. Legal validation isn't just about complying with regulations; it's about safeguarding your property rights. To make this concept more tangible, we'll introduce a real-world example that demonstrates the practical implications of legal validation, showing how it can serve as both a shield and a sword in the realm of Indian real estate.

Important Questions to Ponder:

In the realm of real estate, where each transaction is a mosaic woven with legal intricacies, it is imperative to pause and ponder upon certain crucial questions:

Do you have a clear understanding of the role and significance of each of these documents in a property transaction?

How can knowledge of these documents protect you from potential legal and financial pitfalls?

Have you ensured the authenticity and legality of the documents provided by the seller?

A = Authentication: The Assurance of Legitimacy

In our ongoing exploration of KAGAZ, we now arrive at the second letter, 'A', which stands for Authentication. Imagine this letter as the stamp of legitimacy, the seal of approval and the guardian of your real estate journey. In this chapter, we'll explore deep into the importance of Authentication in property deals, unveiling its significance, sharing real-life stories and equipping you with the knowledge to protect your investments.

Why Authentication Matters:

Authentication is the backbone of trust in the world of real estate. It's the assurance that what you see is what you get, that the promises made are promises kept and that your investment is secure and legitimate. Every document, signature and seal of approval in the world of real estate seeks to establish and confirm the authenticity of a property transaction.

Authentication and the Power of Legitimacy:

Let's begin our journey into the realm of Authentication by understanding its power through the lens of legitimacy. In the world of real estate, legitimacy is the currency of trust. It's what separates a sound investment from a risky proposition.

Imagine the story of Mr and Mrs Kapoor, a young couple who had diligently saved for years to buy their first home. They found a charming apartment in a newly constructed building and everything seemed perfect. However, when they started scrutinising the documents, they noticed a discrepancy in the builder's signature on the Sale Deed. Suspecting foul play, they initiated an Authentication process that revealed the Sale Deed was indeed forged. The Kapoors' vigilance saved them from a potentially devastating financial loss and legal entanglements.

As you embark on your property venture, consider these vital questions:

- Do you truly understand the importance of Authentication in property deals?
  Authentication is more than a formality; it's the guardian of your investment.

- How can a strong Authentication process safeguard you from potential fraud and deceit?
  In a world where risks lurk in every corner, Authentication is your armour.

- Have you ever encountered a situation where Authentication played a pivotal role in a property transaction?
  Real-life stories often carry the most compelling lessons.

The Role of Government Authorities:

In the world of Authentication, government authorities play a pivotal role. They are the gatekeepers of legitimacy, responsible for verifying the authenticity of property documents and transactions. The involvement of government authorities provides an added layer of security to your property deals.

Consider the case of Mr Khan, an investor looking to purchase agricultural land. As he approached the local revenue department to verify the property's ownership, he discovered that the seller had manipulated the documents to show a larger land area than what was actually available. Thanks to the government's Authentication process, the deceit was exposed and Mr Khan avoided a potential scam.

The Do's and Don'ts of Authentication:

- **Do Verify Government Records:** Always cross-verify property details with government records to ensure accuracy and legitimacy.

- **Don't Ignore Red Flags:** If something seems amiss, such as discrepancies in signatures or documents, don't proceed without thorough Authentication.

- **Do Seek Third-Party Authentication:** Consider hiring a third-party expert to conduct due diligence on your behalf, especially for high-value transactions.

- **Don't Rush Transactions:** Take your time to review all documents and ensure their authenticity before committing to a property deal.

Authentication Beyond Documents: The Importance of Due Diligence

While documents are an integral part of Authentication, it goes beyond just paper. Due diligence is a crucial aspect of the Authentication process. It involves conducting thorough research and investigations to ensure that every aspect of a property deal is genuine and transparent.

Imagine the story of Ms Sharma, a single mother looking to buy a flat in a reputed housing society. Everything seemed perfect on paper, but her gut feeling told her to dig deeper. Through due diligence, she uncovered that the builder had failed to obtain the necessary approvals for the construction. This revelation not only saved her from a potentially illegal investment but also exposed the builder's unethical practices.

The Power of Third-Party Authentication:

In some cases, third-party Authentication can provide an additional layer of security. These are independent agencies or professionals who specialise in verifying property transactions. Their impartial assessment can be invaluable in ensuring the legitimacy of a deal.

Consider the scenario of Mr Deshmukh, a businessman looking to purchase a commercial property in a bustling market area. To mitigate risks, he hired a third-party Authentication expert to conduct a thorough review of the documents and the property itself. The expert's findings revealed discrepancies in the property's title, which the seller had concealed. Mr Deshmukh's decision to invest in third-party Authentication not only saved him from a potential financial disaster but also served as a validation of the power of due diligence.

Real Estate Frauds and the Need for Authentication:

Real estate frauds are a harsh reality in the industry. Unscrupulous individuals and entities often prey on unsuspecting buyers and sellers. Without a robust Authentication process, you could fall victim to these fraudulent practices.

Consider the case of Mrs Chatterjee, a widow looking to sell her ancestral property. An individual posing as a buyer approached her and offered a substantial sum in cash. Eager to secure her financial future, Mrs Chatterjee agreed to the deal without proper Authentication. However, after the transaction, she discovered that the currency notes she received were counterfeit. In her desperation,

Mrs Chatterjee had neglected the vital step of Authentication, leading to significant financial loss.

Government Initiatives for Authentication:

To combat fraud and promote transparency in real estate transactions, governments have introduced various initiatives and technologies. These include online portals for document verification, digitisation of land records and the use of blockchain technology to secure property transactions.

Consider the example of the Indian government's DigiLocker initiative, which allows individuals to store and share electronic copies of their documents. This initiative has not only simplified the Authentication process but also reduced the risk of document forgery.

The Wisdom of Authentication:

As we journey through the 'A' of KAGAZ, it becomes evident that Authentication is the sentinel of legitimacy in property transactions. It safeguards your investments, protects your interests and ensures that your real estate journey is free from deceit and fraud.

In the chapters that follow, we will continue our exploration of KAGAZ, delving into the nuances of each element and equipping you with the knowledge and insight necessary for a successful property venture. Remember, Authentication is not just a process; it's your shield in the complex world of real estate, ensuring that every step you take is secure, legitimate and prosperous.

In the words of Benjamin Franklin, "An investment in knowledge pays the best interest." As you explore deeper into the world of Authentication, you're investing in the knowledge that will yield returns in the form of secure and prosperous real estate endeavours.

G = Guardianship:
Understanding Guardianship in Real Estate

"Guardianship is not just about owning property;
it's about protecting your dreams."

Welcome back to our exploration of KAGAZ, where we explore into the vital element represented by 'G' - Guardianship. Imagine Guardianship as the vigilant protector of your real estate interests, standing as the guardian of your investments and the sentinel of your property rights. In this chapter, we will unravel the profound significance of Guardianship in the realm of real estate, using real-life stories and key insights and equipping you with the knowledge to ensure your property ventures are secure and prosperous.

Why Guardianship Matters:

Guardianship in real estate is akin to having a trusted sentinel who watches over your interests, ensuring that your investments remain secure and free from disputes or encroachments. It encompasses various aspects, from property inspections to legal protections, all aimed at safeguarding your property rights.

Consider these fundamental questions as we embark on our exploration of Guardianship:

- Do you truly grasp the significance of Guardianship in real estate? It's more than just paperwork; it's your shield against unforeseen challenges.

- How can a robust Guardianship approach protect you from potential property disputes and losses?
In a world where real estate can be fraught with risks, Guardianship is your safeguard.

- Have you ever encountered a situation where Guardianship played a critical role in resolving a property-related issue?
Real-life stories often hold the most valuable lessons.

Guardianship: The Guardian of Legal Protections

One of the primary facets of Guardianship is the assurance of legal protections in real estate transactions. These protections come in various forms, from property titles to encumbrance certificates, all serving to establish and uphold your property rights.

Imagine the story of Mr and Mrs Rao, a couple who purchased a residential plot in a bustling city with dreams of building their dream home. However, shortly after acquiring the property, they discovered that the land was embroiled in a legal dispute due to unclear title deeds. Legal battles ensued, leading to both financial losses and emotional distress. It was only through persistent legal Guardianship that Mr and Mrs Rao were eventually able to secure their property rights and put an end to the dispute.

The Crown of Legal Guardianship: Property Titles

Property titles are the crown jewel of legal Guardianship in real estate. These documents establish your ownership rights and prove the legitimacy of your property transaction. A clear and unambiguous title is the cornerstone of any secure real estate venture.

Imagine the story of Mr Gupta, a prudent investor looking to purchase a prime commercial property in the heart of the city. He found an ideal property and was ready to proceed with the transaction when his legal advisor raised concerns about the property's title. Further investigation revealed that the property's title was encumbered with multiple legal disputes from the past. Thanks to Mr Gupta's careful consideration and Guardianship, he avoided a potential quagmire of legal challenges and financial losses.

Do's and Don'ts of Legal Guardianship:

- **Do Conduct a Title Search:** Before finalising any property transaction, perform a thorough title search to ensure the property's title is clear and free from encumbrances.

- **Don't Skip Legal Documentation:** Always ensure that all legal documents, such as sale deeds and agreements, are comprehensive and legally sound.

- **Do Consult Legal Experts:** Seek guidance from legal experts or property lawyers to navigate complex legal aspects of real estate transactions.

- **Don't Ignore Property Disputes:** If you encounter property disputes or legal issues, address them promptly and seek legal counsel.

Guardianship and Property Inspections:

Another crucial aspect of Guardianship is property inspections. These inspections involve a thorough examination of the property to identify any structural or legal issues that may affect your investment.

Consider the scenario of Mr Deshmukh, an investor interested in purchasing a commercial property. Despite an attractive offer, he decided to engage a property inspector to assess the building's condition. The inspection revealed structural weaknesses and violations of safety regulations. Thanks to this vigilant approach to Guardianship, Mr Deshmukh avoided a potentially disastrous investment.

Do's and Don'ts of Property Inspections:

- **Do Hire Qualified Inspectors:** Engage professional property inspectors who are experienced in evaluating real estate properties.

- **Don't Rely Solely on Visual Inspections:** Ensure comprehensive inspections that cover structural, electrical, plumbing and other critical aspects of the property.

- **Do Document Inspection Findings:** Maintain a detailed record of inspection findings, including photographs and reports, for future reference.

- **Don't Overlook Legal Compliance:** Verify that the property complies with local building codes and regulations.

Guardianship and Property Disputes:

Property disputes can be a nightmare for real estate investors. Guardianship in this context involves taking preventive measures to reduce the risk of disputes and having strategies in place to resolve them swiftly if they arise.

Consider the case of Mr and Mrs Sharma, a couple who purchased a residential plot for their dream home. Shortly after construction began, a neighbour claimed ownership of a portion of their land, leading to a bitter property dispute. The Sharmas, with the guidance of legal experts, were able to resolve the dispute amicably through negotiations. Their proactive approach to Guardianship allowed them to protect their property rights and avoid protracted legal battles.

Do's and Don'ts of Dealing with Property Disputes:

- **Do Conduct Due Diligence:** Research and investigate the property thoroughly before purchase to identify any potential disputes.

- **Don't Skip Title Insurance:** Consider title insurance to protect yourself against unforeseen property disputes.

- **Do Seek Mediation:** In case of a dispute, consider mediation or negotiation as a first step before resorting to legal action.

- **Don't Delay Resolution:** Act promptly to resolve disputes to prevent escalation and minimise financial losses.

Guardianship and Documentation:

Solid documentation is a cornerstone of effective Guardianship. Keeping comprehensive records of all property-related transactions and communications is essential for protecting your interests.

Imagine the story of Mr Patel, an individual who had purchased a property for investment purposes. Over the years, he accumulated a stack of documents related to the property, including sale deeds, property tax receipts and maintenance records. When a legal issue regarding property boundaries arose, Mr Patel's meticulous record-keeping allowed him to present irrefutable evidence in his favour, ultimately leading to a favourable resolution.

Do's and Don'ts of Property Documentation:

- **Do Maintain a Property File:** Create a dedicated file to store all property-related documents, including purchase agreements, receipts and correspondence.

- **Don't Dispose of Documents:** Retain all property documents, even those that may seem insignificant at the time, as they could be crucial in the future.

- **Do Digitise Documents:** Consider digitising important documents to ensure they are easily accessible and protected from physical damage.

- **Don't Sign Incomplete Agreements:** Read and understand all agreements and contracts thoroughly before signing and seek legal advice if necessary.

Government Regulations and Guardianship:

Government regulations play a significant role in Guardianship. Laws and regulations governing real estate transactions are designed to protect the interests of buyers and sellers.

Consider the example of the Real Estate (Regulation and Development) Act, 2016 (RERA) in India. RERA was enacted to bring transparency and accountability to the real estate sector, ensuring that developers adhere to timelines and provide the promised amenities to buyers. This regulation has significantly enhanced Guardianship for property buyers in India.

The Wisdom of Guardianship:

As we explore deeper into the 'G' of KAGAZ, it becomes evident that Guardianship is the sentinel of your real estate ventures. It safeguards your investments, protects your property rights and ensures that your journey in the world of real estate is secure and prosperous.

In the chapters that follow, we will continue our exploration of KAGAZ, delving into the intricacies of each element and equipping you with the knowledge and insights necessary for successful property ventures. Remember, Guardianship is not just a concept; it's your guardian angel in the complex world of real estate, watching over your investments and ensuring that every step you take is secure, legitimate and fruitful.

In the words of Theodore Roosevelt, "The best prize that life offers is the chance to work hard at work worth doing." Your real estate investments are undoubtedly work worth doing and Guardianship is your key to ensuring that your efforts are rewarded with success and security.

A = Accuracy:
Ensuring Accuracy in Documentation

"Accuracy in documentation is the bridge between intention and realisation in real estate."

In our continuing journey through the labyrinth of KAGAZ, we now arrive at a critical juncture represented by 'A' - Accuracy. If Guardianship stands as the vigilant protector of your real estate interests, Accuracy serves as its trustworthy companion, ensuring that every piece of documentation is precise, truthful and aligned with the reality of your property transaction. In this chapter, we will dive deep into the profound significance of Accuracy in the realm of real estate documentation, fortified by real-life stories, key insights and actionable wisdom to equip you with the knowledge to conduct property deals with precision and confidence.

The Essence of Accuracy:

At its core, Accuracy in real estate documentation is about presenting a truthful and comprehensive account of all aspects of a property transaction. It's not merely about dotting the i's and crossing the t's; it's about painting an accurate portrait of the property, its history and its legal standing.

Let's begin by considering some fundamental questions:

- **Do you truly grasp the significance of Accuracy in property documentation?**
  It's more than just paperwork; it's the cornerstone of trust in real estate deals.

- **How can a commitment to Accuracy protect you from potential disputes, legal complications and financial losses?**
  In a world where real estate transactions involve substantial investments, Accuracy is your insurance against unforeseen pitfalls.

- **Have you ever encountered a situation where inaccuracies or omissions in property documentation had serious consequences?**
  Real-life stories often hold the most compelling lessons.

The Weight of Accuracy:

Accuracy in real estate documentation carries immense weight. It's not a mere formality; it's the bedrock upon which trust between buyers and sellers is built. Inaccuracies or omissions in documents can lead to disputes, financial losses and a tarnished reputation.

Imagine the story of Mr and Mrs Kapoor, a couple who decided to sell their family home to downsize during their retirement. They engaged a real estate agent to manage the sale and trusted them with preparing the property listing. Unfortunately, the agent misrepresented the property's dimensions, resulting in a legal dispute with the buyer. This oversight not only strained the Kapoors' finances but also damaged their trust in the real estate industry. This tale underscores the vital role of Accuracy in property documentation.

> **Do's and Don'ts of Ensuring Accuracy:**
>
> - **Do Verify Property Details:** Cross-check all property details, including dimensions, boundaries and amenities, to ensure they align with reality.
>
> - **Don't Inflate Property Value:** Avoid exaggerating the property's value or potential to attract buyers. Honesty is the best policy.
>
> - **Do Disclose All Relevant Information:** Be transparent about any known issues or defects with the property, ensuring they are clearly mentioned in the documentation.
>
> - **Don't Rely Solely on Oral Agreements:** Always document agreements and understandings in writing to avoid misunderstandings.

Accuracy and Property Descriptions:

Property descriptions play a pivotal role in real estate transactions. Buyers rely on these descriptions to make informed decisions and inaccuracies can lead to misunderstandings and disputes.

Consider the scenario of Mr Desai, a buyer interested in an apartment listed as having 'spectacular sea views'. Trusting the description, Mr Desai made the purchase only to realise that the view was partially obstructed. The inaccurate property description not only left Mr Desai disappointed but also strained his relationship with the seller. This example highlights the importance of providing precise and truthful property descriptions.

> **Do's and Don'ts of Property Descriptions:**
>
> - **Do Use Precise Language:** Describe the property accurately, avoiding hyperbole or exaggeration.
>
> - **Don't Omit Negative Details:** Include any known issues or limitations of the property in the description.

> - **Do Provide Visual Documentation:** Whenever possible, supplement property descriptions with photographs or videos to give buyers a clear understanding.
>
> - **Don't Make Assumptions:** Stick to the facts and avoid making assumptions about a property's potential.

Accuracy and Legal Documentation:

Accuracy is especially crucial in legal documentation, where any discrepancies or inaccuracies can have far-reaching legal consequences. This applies to documents such as sale deeds, contracts and agreements.

Imagine the story of Ms Reddy, an NRI selling her ancestral property in India. To facilitate the sale, she entrusted a lawyer to prepare the sale deed. Unfortunately, the lawyer made an error in specifying the property boundaries, leading to a legal dispute between Ms Reddy and the buyer. This situation not only caused Ms Reddy financial loss but also tarnished her reputation. It underscores the need for rigorous accuracy in legal documentation.

> **Do's and Don'ts of Legal Documentation:**
>
> - **Do Consult Legal Experts:** Seek guidance from experienced property lawyers to ensure all legal documents are accurate and legally sound.
>
> - **Don't Rush the Process:** Take the time to review legal documents carefully before signing and seek legal advice if necessary.
>
> - **Do Verify Ownership Details:** Double-check property ownership details, especially in sale deeds, to ensure they align with reality.
>
> - **Don't Ignore Legal Compliance:** Ensure all legal documents comply with local laws and regulations.

Accuracy and Property History:

A crucial aspect of Accuracy is documenting the property's history accurately. This includes information about previous owners, any legal disputes or changes in property boundaries.

Consider the case of Mr Gupta, who purchased a historical property intending to convert it into a boutique hotel. During the due diligence process, he discovered that the property's history, as presented in the documentation, was inaccurate. It failed to mention past legal disputes over property boundaries. Mr Gupta's commitment to Accuracy led him to investigate further, uncovering the true history of the property. Armed with this knowledge, he was able to navigate the legal complexities and protect his investment.

Do's and Don'ts of Documenting Property History:

- **Do Research Property History:** Investigate the property's history thoroughly, including relevant documents from all the past owners, disputes and boundary changes.

- **Don't Omit Relevant Information:** Include all known historical details in property documentation, ensuring transparency.

- **Do Keep Records:** Maintain a detailed record of the property's history, including any changes or modifications.

- **Don't Make Assumptions:** Base property history documentation on verified facts, not assumptions.

Accuracy and Property Inspections:

Property inspections are a critical aspect of Accuracy. During inspections, it's essential to document the property's condition accurately to avoid disputes later.

Consider the scenario of Mr and Mrs Sharma, who purchased a residential property with a swimming pool. The property inspector failed to note visible cracks in the pool's foundation during the inspection. After moving in, the Sharmas encountered extensive pool repair costs due to the oversight. Accurate documentation of the pool's condition during inspection could have protected them from unexpected expenses.

Do's and Don'ts of Property Inspections:

- **Do Hire Qualified Inspectors:** Engage professional property inspectors with a track record of accuracy.

- **Don't Rush Inspections:** Allow inspectors ample time to thoroughly examine the property.

- **Do Document Inspection Findings:** Maintain detailed records, including photographs, of all inspection findings.

- **Don't Overlook Minor Details:** Even seemingly minor issues should be documented to ensure complete Accuracy.

Accuracy and Property Transactions:

During property transactions, Accuracy is paramount in all interactions, including negotiations, agreements and financial dealings.

Imagine the story of Mr Patel, who negotiated a property purchase with a seller. They reached an oral agreement, with both parties understanding the terms and conditions. However, when it came time to finalise the agreement in writing, discrepancies arose, leading to a dispute. An accurately documented agreement from the beginning could have prevented this situation.

> **Do's and Don'ts of Property Transactions:**
>
> - **Do Record All Agreements:** Ensure that all agreements, whether oral or written, are accurately recorded from the outset.
>
> - **Don't Rely Solely on Memory:** Avoid relying on memory for agreements made during negotiations.
>
> - **Do Seek Legal Advice:** Consult legal experts when drafting or finalising property transaction agreements.
>
> - **Don't Skip Due Diligence:** Conduct thorough due diligence before entering into any property transaction.

Accuracy and Your Reputation:

Your commitment to Accuracy in property transactions not only safeguards your interests but also upholds your reputation in the real estate industry. Word of mouth is a powerful force and honesty and precision in your dealings can lead to positive recommendations and long-lasting relationships.

Accuracy and the Future:

As you navigate the intricate world of real estate, remember that Accuracy is not just about the present; it's an investment in your future. Accurate documentation today can prevent disputes, losses and legal complications tomorrow. It is your assurance that your real estate journey is built on a solid foundation of truth and transparency.

Conclusion:

In our exploration of 'A' - Accuracy in the KAGAZ framework, we have explored into its profound significance and the critical role it plays in ensuring successful and secure property transactions. Accuracy is the beacon of truth that guides you through the labyrinth of real estate documentation, protecting your investments, your reputation and your future.

As we move forward in this journey through KAGAZ, we will continue to unravel the intricacies of each element, equipping you with the knowledge and insights necessary for prosperous property ventures. Remember, Accuracy is not just a concept; it's your ally in the complex world of real estate, ensuring that every document you sign, every property you invest in and every transaction you undertake is grounded in truth and precision.

Z = Zeal: The Zeal for Updates - Staying Current in Property Paperwork

"In the pursuit of property, zeal for updates is the engine of progress."

In our journey through KAGAZ, we arrive at the letter 'Z', representing Zeal. This chapter focuses on the importance of staying current in property paperwork, an often overlooked aspect of real estate transactions. Zeal, in this context, is the unwavering enthusiasm and diligence required to keep all property documentation up-to-date and aligned with the ever-evolving legal and regulatory landscape. Through this chapter, we will explore why maintaining zeal for updates is vital and we will provide you with essential insights, real-life stories, actionable tips and the significance of being proactive in property paperwork.

Understanding the Zeal for Updates:

Staying current in property paperwork is akin to tending to a thriving garden. Neglecting it can result in weeds of complications, disputes and financial losses overgrowing your real estate investments. In contrast, consistent care and attention bear the fruits of hassle-free transactions and secure ownership.

Let's begin our exploration by considering some fundamental questions:

- **Do you recognise the importance of maintaining zeal for updates in property documentation?**
  It's more than just keeping files in order; it's about safeguarding your investments.

- **How can proactively updating property paperwork shield you from potential legal and financial pitfalls?**
  In a dynamic real estate environment, zeal for updates is your armour against uncertainties.

- **Have you ever experienced the consequences of neglecting updates in property documentation?**
  Personal experiences often drive home the significance of staying current.

The Dynamics of Zeal for Updates:

Zeal for Updates is a proactive stance in the realm of real estate paperwork. It involves regularly reviewing, amending and aligning property documents with the latest legal and regulatory changes. This practice ensures that your property dealings remain legally sound and free from complications.

Consider the scenario of Mr Sharma, a property owner who inherited a piece of land from his grandfather. For decades, the land remained unused and property documents lay untouched in an old file. When Mr Sharma decided to develop the land, he discovered that the property's boundaries had been altered due to a municipal road expansion project. His failure to stay current with updates in property paperwork led to legal disputes and significant financial losses. This example underscores the need to maintain zeal for updates.

> **Do's and Don'ts of Zeal for Updates:**
>
> - **Do Regular Document Audits:** Conduct regular audits of your property documents to identify any discrepancies or outdated information.
>
> - **Don't Assume Continuity:** Changes in laws, regulations or property conditions can impact your documents; never assume they remain static.
>
> - **Do Seek Legal Advice:** Consult legal experts or property professionals to ensure your documents comply with current legal standards.
>
> - **Don't Delay Updates:** Promptly address any required updates or amendments to prevent potential issues from escalating.

Zeal for Updates and Property Titles:

Property titles are a core element of real estate transactions. Ensuring that your property title remains current and accurate is essential to protect your ownership rights.

Consider the case of Ms Reddy, who inherited a property but failed to update the title to reflect her ownership. Years later, when she decided to sell the property, potential buyers were deterred by the outdated title. Ms Reddy's lack of zeal for updates resulted in prolonged delays and potential buyers backing out. This situation emphasises the importance of maintaining current property titles.

> **Do's and Don'ts for Property Titles:**
>
> - **Do Update Ownership Titles:** Whenever there is a change in property ownership, update the title to reflect the current owner.
>
> - **Don't Overlook Legal Requirements:** Understand the legal requirements for updating property titles in your jurisdiction.

- **Do Keep Records:** Maintain records of all title updates, including the date and reason for the change.

- **Don't Assume Continuity:** Changes in ownership or property conditions may necessitate updates, even if they seem minor.

Zeal for Updates and Property Tax Records:

Property tax records are another critical aspect of staying current in property paperwork. Failing to update these records can lead to unexpected tax liabilities and legal complications.

Imagine the story of Mr and Mrs Kapoor, who sold their property but neglected to update their property tax records. The tax department continued to send tax notices to their old address, which went unnoticed. Years later, the Kapoors were shocked to discover that they owed a significant amount in unpaid property taxes with penalties. Their failure to maintain zeal for updates in their tax records resulted in a financial burden they had not anticipated.

Do's and Don'ts for Property Tax Records:

- **Do Notify Tax Authorities:** Whenever there is a change in property ownership or address, inform the relevant tax authorities.

- **Don't Ignore Notices:** Regularly check for property tax notices and address any discrepancies promptly.

- **Do Keep Records of Payments:** Maintain records of all property tax payments, including receipts and transaction details.

- **Don't Delay Updates:** Notify tax authorities of any changes without delay to avoid penalties.

Zeal for Updates and Lease Agreements:

Lease agreements require diligent updating, especially when they involve long-term leases. Failure to do so can result in disputes and financial losses.

Consider the case of Mr Patel, who leased a commercial space for his business. Over the years, the rental amount was verbally adjusted, but the lease agreement remained unchanged. When a new landlord took over the property, they demanded the original rent stated in the agreement, leading to a dispute. Mr Patel's lack of zeal for updates in his lease agreement left him in a precarious situation.

Do's and Don'ts for Lease Agreements:

- **Do Document Changes:** If there are any changes in lease terms, ensure they are documented and agreed upon by all parties.

- **Don't Rely on Verbal Agreements:** Avoid relying solely on verbal agreements; all modifications should be in writing.

- **Do Review Lease Terms:** Regularly review lease agreements to ensure they align with the current rental market and conditions.

- **Don't Delay Updates:** Promptly address any required updates or amendments to prevent disputes.

Zeal for Updates and Property Insurance:

Property insurance policies require regular review and updating to ensure adequate coverage and compliance with changing regulations.

Imagine the story of Ms Rao, who purchased property insurance for her home but failed to update the policy when she made significant renovations. When her home suffered damage due to a natural disaster, she discovered that her insurance policy did not cover the updated value of her property. Ms Rao's oversight in maintaining zeal for updates in her insurance policy resulted in inadequate coverage during a critical time.

Do's and Don'ts for Property Insurance:

- **Do Review Coverage:** Regularly review your property insurance policy to ensure it accurately reflects the current value and condition of your property.

- **Don't Overlook Renovations:** Whenever you make substantial changes to your property, update your insurance policy accordingly.

- **Do Consult Insurance Experts:** Seek advice from insurance professionals to ensure your coverage is comprehensive and up-to-date.

- **Don't Delay Updates:** Promptly update your insurance policy to avoid coverage gaps during unexpected events.

The Zeal for Updates and the Future:

In conclusion, the Zeal for Updates is not just a current necessity; it is an investment in your future as a property owner or investor. Regularly reviewing and updating property paperwork, titles, tax records, lease agreements and insurance policies may require time and effort, but the dividends it pays in terms of secure ownership, minimised risks and hassle-free transactions are immeasurable.

As you continue your journey through the intricate world of real estate, remember that zeal for updates is your proactive approach to navigating the dynamic landscape. It safeguards your investments, protects your interests and ensures that your property dealings remain transparent and legally sound.

In the chapters that follow, we will further explore the nuances of each aspect of KAGAZ, equipping you with the knowledge, wisdom and enthusiasm required for successful property ventures. Remember, Zeal for Updates is not just a concept; it's your commitment to excellence in the ever-evolving world of real estate documentation.

In this chapter we have embarked on a profound exploration of the essential cornerstone of real estate transactions: documentation. We have unravelled the intricacies of **KAGAZ, a comprehensive framework that encompasses Knowledge of Necessary Documents (K), Authentication (A), Guardianship (G), Accuracy (A) and Zeal (Z).** This chapter has been a voyage of enlightenment, equipping you with the knowledge and wisdom needed to navigate the labyrinth of property paperwork.

The Wisdom of KAGAZ:

As we conclude this chapter, it is vital to reflect upon the wisdom of KAGAZ. It is more than just paper; it's the compass guiding you through the complex terrain of real estate. KAGAZ empowers you to make informed decisions, protect your interests and navigate property transactions with confidence.

Knowledge of Necessary Documents (K): We began our journey by acquainting you with the essential documents that underpin every property transaction. These documents are the foundation upon which your real estate aspirations are built. From Title Deeds to Property Tax Receipts, you have learned the significance of each document and how they shape the course of property deals.

Authentication (A): In the pursuit of secure property dealings, we emphasised the importance of authenticating property documents. By verifying their origins, integrity and legality, you become the guardian of your interests, ensuring that your transactions remain transparent and trustworthy.

Guardianship (G): We explored the concept of appointing trustworthy individuals as guardians to protect your interests in property transactions. Understanding the role of guardianship ensures that your investments are secure and your dealings are free from deceit.

Accuracy (A): Maintaining the accuracy of property documentation emerged as a key pillar of KAGAZ. By keeping property titles, tax records, lease agreements and insurance policies up-to-date, you secure your financial interests and protect against disputes.

Zeal (Z): Finally, we discussed the importance of zeal for updates in property paperwork. Staying current in your documentation ensures that your investments remain robust and future-proof, adapting to changing circumstances and legal requirements.

The Benefits for Regular Buyers, Sellers and Investors:

This chapter has not only enriched your understanding but also bestowed several invaluable benefits upon regular buyers, sellers and investors in the real estate market:

Confidence: You can approach property transactions with confidence, knowing that you understand the essential documentation involved.

Risk Mitigation: The insights provided help you identify and mitigate potential legal and financial risks.

Legitimate Deals: You can ensure that your property dealings are legitimate, transparent and secure.

Proactive Approach: With a proactive approach to property paperwork, you can safeguard your investments.

Avoiding Pitfalls: Knowledge of the do's and don'ts helps you avoid common pitfalls in real estate transactions.

Clarity in Ownership: You gain clarity regarding property ownership, ensuring that you are buying or selling a legally recognised asset.

Legal Compliance: Understanding property documentation ensures that your transactions adhere to legal and regulatory requirements.

Protection of Interests: The wisdom of KAGAZ helps you appoint trustworthy guardians to protect your interests in property dealings.

Financial Security: By maintaining accurate documentation, you secure your financial interests and avoid disputes.

Future-Proofing: Regular updates and reviews of property paperwork future-proof your investments, ensuring their long-term viability.

The KAGAZ Checklist:

Before we conclude this chapter, here is a detailed KAGAZ checklist that you can use as a reference in your property transactions:

Knowledge of Necessary Documents (K):

Title Deed:

- ❏ Verify the clarity, ownership and encumbrance status of the property's Title Deed.
- ❏ Ensure the Title Deed matches the seller's identity.
- ❏ Confirm the absence of any legal disputes or pending dues related to the property.
- ❏ Check if there are any previous mortgages or loans against the property.
- ❏ Ensure that the Title Deed is clear and free of any ambiguities.

Sale Deed:

- ❏ Ensure that the Sale Deed is executed on a non-judicial stamp paper.
- ❏ Confirm that the Sale Deed facilitates a legitimate transfer of ownership.
- ❏ Verify that the Sale Deed includes all essential property details.
- ❏ Check if the Sale Deed specifies any conditions or clauses that may affect the transaction.
- ❏ Ensure that the Sale Deed is registered with the relevant authority.

Encumbrance Certificate:

- ❏ Confirm that the property is free from legal and financial liabilities.
- ❏ Verify that the Encumbrance Certificate covers the required period.

- Check for any encumbrances or charges on the property, such as mortgages or liens.
- Investigate if there are any legal disputes or pending litigation related to the property.
- Ensure that the Encumbrance Certificate is obtained from the appropriate authority.

Khata Certificate and Extract:

- Check if the property has a Khata certificate and extract, as required by local regulations.
- Verify that the Khata details match the property's ownership and dimensions.
- Confirm the Khata transfer process if necessary.
- Check for any pending property tax dues associated with the property.
- Ensure that the Khata certificate is issued in the correct category (A, B or C).

Occupancy Certificate:

- For multi-story buildings, ensure the presence of an Occupancy Certificate.
- Verify that the certificate is issued by the local municipal authority.
- Confirm that the building complies with the approved building plan.
- Check if there are any deviations from the approved plan in the Occupancy Certificate.
- Ensure that the Occupancy Certificate includes the property's address and details.

Building Approval Plan:

- ☐ Validate that the property complies with approved building plans and safety standards.

- ☐ Check for any deviations from the approved plan in the Building Approval Plan.

- ☐ Confirm that the Building Approval Plan is in line with local regulations.

- ☐ Investigate if there are any zoning or land-use restrictions applicable to the property.

- ☐ Ensure that the Building Approval Plan includes structural details and specifications.

Power of Attorney:

- ☐ Exercise caution when granting or receiving Power of Attorney for property transactions.

- ☐ Ensure that the Power of Attorney document clearly defines the scope of authority.

- ☐ Verify the authenticity of the Power of Attorney document.

- ☐ Check if the Power of Attorney is irrevocable or revocable as per the terms.

- ☐ Confirm that the Power of Attorney is duly notarised and registered if required by law.

Building Completion Certificate:

- ☐ Confirm the property's completion according to the approved plan.

- ☐ Check for any discrepancies between the completed structure and the plan.

- ☐ Ensure that the Building Completion Certificate is issued by the appropriate authority.

- ☐ Verify that the certificate includes details about the property's construction date.

- ☐ Investigate if there are any outstanding construction-related violations or penalties.

Property Tax Receipts:

- ☐ Verify that property taxes are up to date to avoid unexpected financial burdens.

- ☐ Confirm that all property tax payments are made by the seller up to the date of the transaction.

- ☐ Ensure that there are no pending property tax dues.

- ☐ Investigate if there are any special assessments or additional taxes associated with the property.

- ☐ Check if property tax assessments are based on the correct property valuation.

Authentication (A):

Document Authentication:

- ☐ Verify the authenticity of all property documents by cross-referencing with official records and authorities.

- ☐ Confirm that the documents have not been tampered with or forged.

- ☐ Check the legitimacy of signatures and seals on documents.

- ☐ Investigate if there are any duplicate or counterfeit documents in circulation.

- ☐ Ensure that all property documents are in compliance with local and national regulations.

Identity Authentication:

- Authenticate the identity of all parties involved in the transaction.
- Ensure that the seller's identity matches the details on the property documents.
- Verify the identity of witnesses, if any, on property documents.
- Confirm the identity of the notary or authorised signatories on legal documents.
- Investigate if there are any cases of identity theft or impersonation related to the property.

Power of Attorney Authentication:

- Confirm the legitimacy of any Power of Attorney documents.
- Verify the identity and authority of the person granted Power of Attorney.
- Ensure that the Power of Attorney is duly registered if required by law.
- Check for any discrepancies between the Power of Attorney and the actual authority granted.
- Investigate if there are any cases of fraudulent Power of Attorney used in property transactions.

Guardianship (G):

Appointment of Guardians:

- Appoint trustworthy individuals as guardians to protect your interests in property transactions.
- Clearly define the scope of authority for guardians to avoid disputes.

- Ensure that guardians are aware of their responsibilities and act in your best interest.
- Check the background and reputation of potential guardians to prevent conflicts of interest.
- Investigate if there are any legal disputes or challenges related to the guardianship of the property.

Accuracy (A):

Regular Review and Updates:

- Regularly review and update property titles, tax records, lease agreements and insurance policies.
- Keep all property-related records accurate and up to date.
- Correct any inaccuracies or discrepancies in property documentation promptly.
- Monitor changes in property laws and regulations that may require updates to your documents.
- Investigate if there are any cases of fraudulent alterations or misrepresentations in property records.

Zeal (Z):

Stay Informed:

- Stay informed about changes in property laws, regulations and tax policies.
- Periodically review and update property documentation to adapt to changing circumstances.
- Stay vigilant about updates and amendments in property-related legislation.

- [ ]   Consider seeking legal counsel or expert advice to stay current with property-related matters.

- [ ]   Investigate if there are any emerging trends or technologies that can enhance your property documentation and management practices.

As we venture beyond the boundaries of KAGAZ, we stand at the precipice of a new frontier: KABZA. In the upcoming chapters, we'll plunge into the intricacies of legal possession, a world where ownership takes shape, boundaries are defined and your property becomes an extension of your rights and dreams.

Just as KAGAZ illuminated the path to prudent property documentation, KABZA will serve as your guiding star in the realm of property possession. It will unveil the layers of complexity surrounding the concept of rightful ownership, providing you with the tools to secure your property with confidence.

So, brace yourself for an enlightening journey through the intricacies of real estate possession. Stay with us as we embark on this expedition, for there is much more to discover and unravel on this captivating path.

"Precision in documentation is not just a safeguard; it is the key to unlocking the true value of your property. By mastering the art of thorough record-keeping, we not only protect our investments but also pave the way for future growth and prosperity."

Chapter 4

KABZA - Safeguarding Your Property Rights

K = Empowering with Knowledge of Rights

In the intricate web of real estate transactions, knowledge is your most potent weapon. It's the beacon that illuminates the path to securing your property rights and making informed decisions. In this section of 'KAGAZ & KABZA', we explore into the significance of empowering yourself with knowledge and understanding your property rights in India.

The Right to Ownership:

At the heart of property rights is the fundamental right to ownership. This right ensures that you have legal control over your property, granting you the authority to use, enjoy and dispose of it as you see fit. In essence, it forms the bedrock of real estate transactions, whether you're buying, selling or inheriting property.

Ownership of property can take various forms, including freehold and leasehold. A freehold property means that you have absolute ownership and you can hold onto it indefinitely. On the other hand, a leasehold property involves ownership for a predetermined period, after which it may revert to the landowner.

Understanding this right is crucial because it dictates how you can exercise your control over the property. For instance, if you're purchasing a residential property, you have the right to live in it, lease it or sell it. However, if you're buying agricultural land, your rights may be limited to farming activities.

The Right to Transfer:

One of the key aspects of property rights is the right to transfer your property. This means that you can sell, gift or bequest your property to someone else. However, there are essential considerations when exercising this right.

For instance, when selling a property, you must follow the legal procedures for transferring ownership. This typically involves drafting a sale deed, obtaining the necessary approvals and ensuring that the property has a clear title. It's crucial to understand the tax implications of property transfers, as these can vary based on factors such as the property's value and your relationship with the transferee.

Additionally, when gifting or bequeathing property, understanding the implications of such transactions is vital. Property gifts often have tax implications and wills or inheritance documents must comply with legal requirements to ensure a smooth transfer of ownership.

The Right to Enjoyment:

Property rights also encompass the right to enjoy your property without interference. This means that you have the liberty to use your property as you see fit, as long as it doesn't violate any laws or regulations.

For instance, if you own a residential apartment, you have the right to live in it, decorate it and even rent it out for additional income. However, you must adhere to the local laws and housing society regulations to avoid disputes. These regulations can cover aspects such as noise levels, parking and property alterations.

The Right to Exclusion:

Property ownership comes with the right to exclude others from your property without your permission. In other words, you can decide who can enter or use your property. However, there are exceptions to this right, such as legal authorities' ability to enter your property with proper authorisation.

Understanding these rights forms the foundation of your property knowledge. With this knowledge, you can make informed decisions, safeguard your rights and protect your property from potential disputes and encroachments.

Empowering Through Knowledge: A Real-Life Story

To illustrate the power of knowledge in property rights, let's meet Rajesh and Meera, a couple living in Mumbai, India. They decided to invest in a plot of land on the outskirts of the city to build their dream home.

As they embarked on this journey, they recognised the importance of understanding their property rights. They researched the property thoroughly, ensuring that it had a clear title, no pending disputes and all necessary approvals from local authorities. They also hired a legal expert to review the sale deed and verify its authenticity.

Their diligence paid off. Armed with knowledge, Rajesh and Meera confidently acquired the land and began construction on their dream home. They navigated the complexities of property ownership with ease and their investment remained secure.

This real-life story underscores the significance of knowledge in property rights. By empowering themselves with information, Rajesh and Meera protected their interests and ensured a smooth real estate transaction.

Do's And Don'ts For Empowering With Knowledge Of Rights

Do's:

- **Research Thoroughly:** Before Investing In Any Property, Conduct Extensive Research To Understand Its History, Title And Any Legal Issues Associated With It.

- **Seek Legal Advice:** Consult With A Qualified Legal Expert Who Specialises In Real Estate To Review Documents And Provide Guidance.

- **Stay Informed:** Keep Yourself Updated On Property Laws, Regulations And Local Rules That May Affect Your Rights As A Property Owner.

Don'ts:

- **Rush Into Transactions:** Avoid Hasty Decisions. Take The Time To Review Documents And Conduct Due Diligence To Protect Your Rights.

- **Ignore Legal Procedures:** Always Follow Legal Procedures When Transferring Property. Skipping Steps Can Lead To Future Complications.

- **Overlook Local Regulations:** Be Aware Of And Comply With Local Housing Society Rules, Zoning Regulations And Land-Use Policies To Prevent Disputes.

By following these do's and don'ts and empowering yourself with knowledge, you can navigate the complex landscape of property rights with confidence and ensure that your real estate investments are secure and legally sound.

Connecting the Dots:

Empowering yourself with knowledge of property rights is the first step toward safeguarding your real estate investments. Understanding your right to ownership, transfer, enjoyment and exclusion ensures that you can make informed decisions and protect your interests. In the next section, we'll explore the intricacies of property agreements and how they play a crucial role in securing your property rights in India.

In this fascinating journey of real estate exploration, knowledge truly is power. As we've witnessed through Rajesh and Meera's story, it can be the difference between a successful, secure investment and a potential legal quagmire. So, let's continue our expedition, armed with the understanding of property rights, as we explore into the world of property agreements.

Types of Property Ownership:

Property ownership in India takes on various forms, each with its unique nuances and legal implications. Delving into these types of ownership is like uncovering hidden treasures within the real estate landscape:

- **Joint Ownership:** Imagine a family coming together to share the ownership of a property, a beautiful ancestral home, perhaps. Joint ownership is a collective decision-making, but to ensure its beauty endures, clear terms and agreements must be established.

- **Ancestral Property:** An ancestral property carries the echoes of generations past. It's governed by laws like the Hindu Succession Act and others and its significance is etched deeply into family histories. Understanding the rights of heirs and co-owners is akin to preserving a priceless legacy.

- **Tenancy Rights:** Picture a rented house or apartment—someone's temporary haven. Tenants have specific legal rights, ensuring they dwell in safe and comfortable surroundings. Landlords also have rights and responsibilities, like maintaining the property and upholding the terms of the rental agreement.

Property Rights in Different States:

Property laws in India are woven with regional variations. Each state contributes its unique colours and patterns to this legal fabric:

- **Property Registration:** The process and requirements for property registration are akin to unique rituals in different states. By understanding these rituals, you ensure your property complies with local customs.

- **Stamp Duty:** Picture stamp duty rates as musical notes, creating distinct melodies in each state. Paying the right notes ensures a harmonious legal composition.

- **Land Ceiling Laws:** Imagine land ceiling laws as geographical boundaries. Each state's boundaries may vary, affecting property transactions in ways as diverse as the landscapes themselves.

Legal Procedures for Property Transactions:

Navigating the legal procedures involved in property transactions is like embarking on a grand adventure.

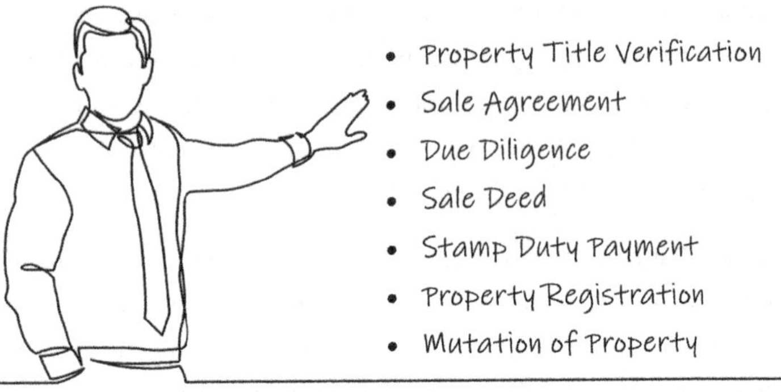

- **Property Title Verification:** Your journey begins with a quest to verify the title of the property, ensuring it's free from encumbrances, liens or legal disputes.

- **Sale Agreement:** Envision a contract signed under the clear sky, outlining all terms and conditions of the property transaction. It's your treasure map, leading you to the promised land.

- **Due Diligence:** Think of due diligence as the careful examination of your treasure map, verifying its authenticity and following the path it lays out.

- **Sale Deed:** The sale deed is the ultimate treasure chest, containing the keys to your new property. Once you possess it, you're the legal owner.

- **Stamp Duty Payment:** The stamp duty payment is your contribution to the legal orchestra, ensuring the transaction's legality and harmony.

- **Property Registration:** Registering your property is akin to planting your flag in a new land, marking it as your own. It's an essential step in your adventure.

- **Mutation of Property:** Imagine updating your map with newfound landmarks. Mutating your property records ensures your treasure is accurately marked on the map of the world.

Challenges and Pitfalls:

The real estate journey in India is not without its challenges—a series of obstacles and hidden traps await:

- **Land Disputes**: Picture land disputes as formidable dragons guarding their hoards. These disputes often involve boundary conflicts or competing claims and can lead to prolonged legal battles.

- **Encroachments**: Envision encroachments as creeping vines, slowly overtaking your property. Unauthorised encroachments can spark legal conflicts that threaten your ownership.

- **Legal Battles**: Engaging in legal battles is like navigating treacherous waters. It's essential to steer clear of these stormy seas whenever possible or seek safe harbours when necessary.

- **Documentation Errors**: Imagine documentation errors as riddles in an ancient script. Solving these riddles ensures your treasure remains intact.

Property Rights in Succession Planning:

Property rights in India can be compared to a legacy, passed down through generations. Planning for this succession is akin to writing a captivating epic:

- **Ensuring Smooth Succession**: A well-drafted will is like an enchanted scroll, ensuring your property transitions seamlessly to the next generation.

- **Tax Planning**: Think of tax planning as a magical potion, concocted to minimise tax burdens for your heirs, preserving their wealth.

- **Protecting Family Interests**: Your will is a guardian, protecting the interests and financial security of your loved ones long after your journey ends.

A = Understanding of Agreements: Making Informed Decisions

In the intricate tapestry of property rights, understanding agreements is akin to deciphering ancient scrolls filled with cryptic symbols. These agreements are the foundation of every property transaction in India and comprehending them is your key to making informed decisions and ensuring a secure investment. As we unravel the mysteries of 'KABZA', let's embark on a journey to grasp the significance of understanding property agreements.

The Importance of Property Agreements:

Property agreements are the pillars upon which property transactions stand. They outline the terms, conditions and obligations that bind buyers, sellers, landlords and tenants. These agreements come in various forms, such as sale deeds, lease agreements and rental contracts and they play a pivotal role in safeguarding the interests of all parties involved.

Imagine you're purchasing your dream home, a spacious apartment in a bustling metropolis. The excitement is palpable as you sign the sale agreement, the document that lays out the terms of the transaction. However, without a clear understanding of the agreement's clauses, you may find yourself in murky waters. What if there are hidden costs, undisclosed liabilities or ambiguous terms? Without proper comprehension, you risk making decisions that could have far-reaching consequences.

Challenges in Understanding Agreements:

The challenges of understanding property agreements are akin to navigating a labyrinth with hidden traps. Many individuals, in their eagerness to secure a property, rush through the agreement-signing process without comprehending the legal jargon and implications. This haste can lead to misunderstandings, disputes and financial setbacks down the road.

Common challenges include:

- **Legal Language:** Property agreements are often laden with legal terminology that can be perplexing to the uninitiated. Phrases like 'force majeure', 'covenants' and 'indemnification' can seem like a foreign language.

- **Hidden Clauses:** Critical clauses buried within the agreement may go unnoticed. These clauses can pertain to maintenance responsibilities, dispute resolution mechanisms or penalty clauses.

- **Financial Implications:** Failure to understand the financial implications of the agreement can lead to unexpected expenses. These may include maintenance charges, property taxes or penalties for default.

A Real-Life Tale of Informed Decision-Making:

Meet Arjun and Sneha, a couple from Bangalore, India, who are on a quest to find their ideal home. After months of searching, they finally stumbled upon a charming villa in a gated community. Excitement mingled with apprehension as they prepared to sign the purchase agreement.

Instead of rushing through the process, Arjun and Sneha decided to seek clarity. They engaged the services of a legal expert to dissect the agreement and explain its intricacies. This decision proved to be their wisest move.

During the review, the legal expert pointed out clauses related to maintenance charges and property taxes that Arjun and Sneha had overlooked. Armed with this knowledge, they renegotiated the terms with the seller, leading to a more favourable agreement. Their understanding of the agreement not only saved them money but also ensured a smooth and transparent transaction.

Do's And Don'ts For Understanding Agreements:

Do's:

Seek Professional Assistance: Engage A Qualified Legal Expert Or Real Estate Advisor To Review Property Agreements. Their Expertise Can Provide Valuable Insights And Prevent Potential Pitfalls.

Read Thoroughly: Take The Time To Read The Agreement Thoroughly. Pay Attention To Every Clause And Seek Clarification On Anything That Seems Unclear.

> **Negotiate When Necessary:** Don't hesitate to negotiate terms that you find unfavourable. Many agreements are open to negotiation and a fair compromise can benefit both parties.
>
> **Don'ts:**
>
> **Rush the Process:** Avoid the temptation to rush through the agreement-signing process. Patience and due diligence are your allies.
>
> **Ignore Legal Advice:** Disregarding legal advice can lead to costly mistakes. Always consider the recommendations of legal experts.
>
> **Overlook Financial Implications:** Property agreements often involve financial commitments. Ignoring these implications can lead to unforeseen expenses.

The Connection to Other Elements of KABZA:

Understanding property agreements is the bridge that connects various elements of 'KABZA'. Your knowledge of property agreements is intertwined with your rights as a property owner or tenant. It also plays a crucial role in establishing clear boundaries and aiming for zero discrepancies in property ownership.

Property agreements dictate your responsibilities and rights concerning the property. They define the boundaries of your ownership and specify the terms of your relationship with other parties involved. Furthermore, your comprehension of these agreements is essential to ensure a secure safety net, as it helps you avoid legal pitfalls and financial setbacks.

The Real-Life Impact of Informed Decision-Making:

Arjun and Sneha's story underscores the profound impact of understanding property agreements. Their willingness to seek expert guidance and grasp the intricacies of the agreement not only protected their interests but also enhanced their overall property-buying experience.

By demystifying the complex language of property agreements, you empower yourself to make informed decisions, negotiate effectively and safeguard your investments. Every clause in an agreement becomes a stepping stone toward securing your property rights and financial well-being.

Unlocking the Full Potential of Informed Decision-Making:

While the importance of understanding agreements cannot be overstated, the journey to becoming an informed property owner involves much more. In the subsequent sections of 'KABZA', we'll explore additional facets of property rights, including establishing clear boundaries, aiming for zero discrepancies in property ownership and ensuring a robust safety net.

As our expedition through the world of property rights continues, remember that every piece of knowledge you gain is a powerful tool in your arsenal. The more you understand, the more secure and confident you become in navigating the intricate realm of real estate. Stay with us on this enlightening journey, where every chapter brings you closer to becoming a master of your property destiny.

Avoiding Pitfalls in Property Agreements: Your Guide to Informed Decision-Making

Property agreements are crucial legal documents that govern the rights and responsibilities of parties involved in real estate transactions. Whether you're purchasing, selling or leasing property in India, it's essential to be aware of potential pitfalls that can arise in property agreements. This article provides a detailed exploration of these pitfalls, complete with case studies and expert advice, to empower Indian readers with the knowledge to make informed decisions and protect their interests.

1. Vague Clauses:

Vague or ambiguous clauses in property agreements can lead to disputes and legal complications. For instance, unclear descriptions of the property, usage restrictions or maintenance responsibilities can create confusion. A notable case is Noida's very popular developer's housing projects, where vague terms led to delays and dissatisfaction among homebuyers.

Case Study: In 2019, the National Consumer Disputes Redressal Commission (NCDRC) ordered developers to compensate homebuyers due to inadequate and vague clauses in their agreements.

Solution: Ensure precise and detailed descriptions of the property and clearly outline usage rights and maintenance obligations. Engage legal experts to review and draft unambiguous clauses.

2. One-Sided Agreements:

Imbalanced property agreements that favour one party over the other can result in unfair outcomes. Buyers or tenants may find themselves with limited rights and excessive burdens, while sellers or landlords might face difficulties in enforcing their terms.

Case Study: The 2017 A leading Infratech Company case involved a large number of homebuyers who were affected by one-sided agreements, leading to significant delays and financial distress.

Solution: Seek legal counsel to ensure a balanced agreement that considers the interests of all parties. Negotiate fair terms regarding payment schedules, penalty clauses and dispute resolution mechanisms.

3. Unclear Terms:

Unclear or poorly defined terms in property agreements can create confusion regarding the parties' obligations and rights. This can result in disputes and legal battles, causing financial losses and stress.

Case Study: The 2018 Supreme Court ruling on the leading steel company case highlighted the importance of clarity in property agreements to avoid legal uncertainties and potential delays.

Solution: Clearly define terms related to payment schedules, possession dates and penalties for breach. Include provisions for potential scenarios like delays or force majeure events.

4. Inadequate Due Diligence:

Failure to conduct thorough due diligence before entering into a property agreement can lead to unforeseen complications. Undisclosed legal disputes, land title issues or zoning restrictions can significantly impact the transaction.

Case Study: An apartment complex in the southern part of Worli in South Mumbai, showcased the repercussions of inadequate due diligence, as residents faced eviction due to unauthorised construction.

Solution: Conduct comprehensive due diligence, including verifying property titles, checking for encumbrances and ensuring compliance with local regulations. Consult legal experts and property professionals to identify potential red flags.

5. Ignoring Local Regulations:

Neglecting to adhere to local laws and regulations can have serious consequences. Zoning restrictions, building codes and environmental requirements must be considered to avoid legal penalties and project disruptions.

Case Study: The famous housing society case of Mumbai highlighted how non-compliance with local regulations can lead to demolition orders and legal actions.

Solution: Familiarise yourself with local laws, zoning regulations and environmental norms. Involve legal experts and engage with local authorities to ensure your property agreement aligns with legal requirements.

Conclusion:

Navigating property agreements in India requires a keen understanding of potential pitfalls and a proactive approach to avoid them. By addressing issues like vague clauses, one-sided agreements, unclear terms, inadequate due diligence and ignoring local regulations, individuals can safeguard their interests and ensure smoother property transactions. Consulting legal experts, conducting thorough due diligence and negotiating balanced terms are essential steps toward creating enforceable and mutually beneficial property agreements.

B = Establishing Clear Boundaries
Respecting the Limits

In the intricate of property ownership, boundaries are the threads that weave together the essence of your ownership. They are not mere lines on the ground but invisible barriers that define the extent of your domain, distinguishing it from your neighbours and the wider world. Establishing clear boundaries is akin to laying the cornerstone for a harmonious and prosperous coexistence with those who share the vicinity.

- **Preventing Conflicts:** The significance of well-defined boundaries cannot be overstated when it comes to averting conflicts with neighbours. In a world where everyone knows where their property begins and ends, disputes stemming from encroachments, land use disagreements or disputes over property lines are far less likely to take root. Clarity begets peace.

- **Legal Certainty:** Clear boundaries offer the priceless gift of legal certainty. They cast a spotlight on the exact extent of your property rights and obligations, empowering you to make informed decisions regarding land use, construction or property development. With clear boundaries, you stand on firm legal ground, minimising uncertainties that can lead to disputes.

- **Property Value:** Property boundaries are intricately tied to the value of your real estate. Prospective buyers or investors are naturally inclined to consider properties with well-marked and uncontested boundaries. Such properties exude a sense of security and assurance that their investments will not be mired in disputes. Thus, establishing clear boundaries becomes an investment in your property's attractiveness and marketability.

Challenges in Establishing Clear Boundaries:

As we explore the importance of clear boundaries, it's crucial to recognise the formidable challenges property owners often face in their pursuit of boundary clarity. These challenges, while daunting, underscore the need for a proactive approach to safeguard property rights:

- **Unclear Land Records:** Indian land records, in many cases, are a quagmire of unreliability, outdated information or glaring omissions. This ambiguity in land records creates a breeding ground for uncertainty and lays the foundation for disputes over property boundaries. Property owners must navigate this minefield with caution.

- **Boundary Disputes:** Boundary conflicts with neighbours can swiftly escalate into contentious legal battles, resulting in strained relationships and financial drain. Such disputes may stem from differences in perception, encroachments by one party or vague property descriptions that leave room for interpretation. Resolving boundary disputes often requires diplomacy and legal expertise.

- **Encroachments:** Unauthorised encroachments onto your property represent a persistent challenge. Neighbours or third parties may gradually extend their structures, fences or activities beyond their rightful boundaries, infringing upon your property. Recognising and addressing encroachments is essential to maintaining the integrity of your property boundaries.

- **Ambiguous Deeds:** Property deeds, while intended to provide clarity, can sometimes introduce ambiguity due to vague or inconsistent boundary descriptions. These ambiguities can result in misunderstandings, conflicts and costly litigation. Property owners must scrutinise deeds meticulously and, if necessary, seek legal clarification.

A Real-Life Tale of Boundary Clarity:

To bring the significance of establishing clear boundaries into sharp focus, consider the inspiring story of Raj and Priya, a couple with a vision of creating their dream home in a serene village in Rajasthan, India. Drawn to the natural beauty of the landscape, they invested their savings in a picturesque piece of land.

However, their dream journey took an unexpected turn when they discovered that the boundaries of their property were not clearly defined and were subject to disputes. Faced with the looming spectre of potential encroachments and boundary conflicts with neighbouring landowners, Raj and Priya made a resolute decision to take a proactive stance.

They enlisted the expertise of a qualified land surveyor, well-versed in the art of accurately demarcating property boundaries. This surveyor's diligent work not only bestowed upon them precise boundary lines but also unveiled a minor encroachment by a neighbouring farmer.

In an assertion of their wisdom, Raj and Priya chose a path of constructive engagement rather than resorting to adversarial legal action. They empathised with the farmer's concerns and extended a hand of assistance to improve his irrigation system. In the spirit of neighbourly cooperation, the farmer reciprocated by agreeing to rectify the encroachment.

This amicable resolution proved to be a triumph, benefitting all parties involved. It prevented the initiation of drawn-out legal battles, preserved harmonious neighbourly relations *and*, most importantly, safeguarded Raj and Priya's property rights. Their story serves as a compelling illustration of the significance of proactive boundary management in preserving property harmony.

Do's and Don'ts for Establishing Clear Boundaries:

Do's:

- **Professional Land Survey:** Prioritise engaging a qualified land surveyor to conduct a professional survey for accurate boundary demarcation. This essential step is the bedrock of boundary clarity.

- **Open Communication:** In cases of boundary disputes or uncertainties, opt for open and respectful communication with neighbouring property owners. Constructive dialogue often paves the way for mutually agreeable solutions that preserve neighbourly relations.

- **Document Agreements:** Whenever an agreement is reached with a neighbour regarding boundaries or encroachments, it is paramount to document the terms in writing. This documentation serves as a critical reference point and a preventative measure against future misunderstandings.

- **Verify Land Records:** Cross-referencing land records with the results of a professional land survey is a prudent practice. It ensures that historical records align with the current status of property boundaries, offering a comprehensive view of the property's extent.

Don'ts:

- **Assume Boundaries:** Never make the assumption that physical features such as fences or walls accurately represent legal boundaries. These structures may not align with the precise property lines.

- **Ignore Encroachments:** In the event of suspected encroachments on your property, avoid the temptation to ignore them. Timely recognition and action are vital to maintaining the integrity of your property boundaries and rights.

- **Rely Solely on Old Records:** While historical land records provide valuable insights, relying solely on them can be risky. They may not always offer a complete and accurate depiction of property boundaries. A professional land survey complements historical records by providing up-to-date information.

The Connection to Other Elements of KABZA:

The establishment of clear boundaries is not an isolated endeavour but a pivotal element that harmonises with other facets of the 'KABZA' framework. Your understanding of property agreements, property rights and the establishment of clear boundaries are interconnected.

In property agreements, clear boundary descriptions are essential to avoid ambiguities and potential disputes. A robust understanding of property rights empowers you to confidently assert your boundaries and address conflicts when they arise.

Furthermore, respecting the limits and boundaries of your property is a critical step in 'Aiming for Zero Discrepancies in Property Ownership'. With clear boundaries, you can readily identify and rectify any discrepancies or encroachments, thus minimising legal and financial risks.

The Holistic Approach to Property Rights:

As you navigate the 'KABZA' framework, remember that each element contributes significantly to the safeguarding of your property rights. Establishing clear boundaries is more than just delineating lines on the ground; it is about acknowledging your responsibility to preserve property harmony, respecting the limits that define your ownership and upholding the legal, ethical and practical boundaries that safeguard your property investment.

In our next chapter, 'Z: Aiming for Zero Discrepancies in Property Ownership', we will explore deeper into the meticulous steps required to ensure that your property ownership remains free from discrepancies and challenges. Stay with us on this enlightening journey, where every chapter brings you closer to becoming a master of your property destiny.

Z = Aiming for Zero Discrepancies in Property Ownership

In the realm of property rights, the aspiration for zero discrepancies in property ownership is not merely a lofty ideal; it's a pragmatic goal that holds immense significance. Property ownership is the cornerstone of one's financial security and legacy and even the slightest discrepancy can lead to unforeseen challenges. As we navigate the multifaceted landscape of 'KABZA', let's explore into the profound importance of aiming for zero discrepancies in property ownership.

The Significance of a Discrepancy-Free Ownership:

A property ownership discrepancy, no matter how minor, can have far-reaching consequences. It can cast doubt on the legitimacy of your property rights, trigger disputes and erode the value of your investment. Achieving zero discrepancies in property ownership is essential for several compelling reasons:

- **Legal Clarity:** Property ownership discrepancies can arise due to inaccuracies in property records, title deeds or survey documents. These inaccuracies can lead to legal disputes and challenges to your ownership rights. Ensuring that your property ownership is free from discrepancies provides you with legal clarity and peace of mind.

- **Financial Security:** Your property often represents a significant portion of your financial portfolio. Any discrepancies in ownership can affect your financial security. For example, if a third party claims ownership of a portion of your property due to a discrepancy, it can lead to financial losses and legal expenses. Zero discrepancies safeguard your financial interests.

- **Smooth Transactions:** Aiming for zero discrepancies simplifies property transactions. When you decide to sell, mortgage or pass on your property, having a clean and undisputed ownership record makes the process smoother and more efficient.

Challenges in Achieving Zero Discrepancies:

While the goal of zero discrepancies in property ownership is paramount, the journey to achieving it is not without its challenges. Property owners often encounter obstacles and uncertainties along the way:

- **Inaccurate Property Records:** Property records in India can be plagued by inaccuracies, inconsistencies and outdated information. This can lead to discrepancies in property ownership that need to be rectified.

- **Legacy Issues:** Inherited properties, especially those passed down through generations, can be riddled with complex ownership issues. Resolving these legacy issues to achieve zero discrepancies can be a daunting task.

- **Boundary Conflicts:** Boundary disputes with neighbours or encroachments onto your property can create discrepancies in ownership boundaries. Resolving these conflicts and restoring accurate property boundaries is crucial.

- **Documentation Errors:** Errors or omissions in property documents, such as sale deeds or inheritance records, can result in discrepancies. These errors may require legal rectification.

A Real-Life Story of Zero Discrepancies:

To illustrate the real-world significance of aiming for zero discrepancies in property ownership, let's explore the story of Anil and Sunita, a couple residing in Chennai, India. They inherited a property from their grandparents, a charming ancestral home with significant sentimental value.

However, when Anil and Sunita decided to renovate the property and pass it on to the next generation, they discovered discrepancies in the property records. The boundaries of their property were inaccurately defined and there were disputes with neighbouring landowners regarding encroachments.

Rather than succumbing to frustration or resorting to adversarial legal battles, Anil and Sunita chose a different path. They engaged a team of qualified surveyors and legal experts to meticulously review the property records, conduct boundary surveys and negotiate with the neighbours.

Through a combination of legal rectification, amicable resolutions and documentation updates, Anil and Sunita successfully eliminated the discrepancies in their property ownership. They transformed their ancestral property into a hassle-free, legally sound asset that they could proudly pass on to the next generation.

Do's and Don'ts for Achieving Zero Discrepancies:

Do's:

- **Conduct Due Diligence:** Before acquiring a property, conduct thorough due diligence to identify any existing discrepancies in ownership or property records.

- **Engage Professionals:** Seek the expertise of qualified surveyors, legal advisors and property experts to rectify discrepancies and ensure accurate ownership records.

> - **Resolve Disputes Amicably:** When encountering boundary disputes or ownership conflicts, explore amicable resolutions and negotiations before resorting to litigation.
>
> **Don'ts:**
>
> - **Ignore Discrepancies:** Ignoring discrepancies in property ownership can lead to future legal and financial complications. Address them proactively.
>
> - **Rush Property Transactions:** Avoid hasty property transactions without proper verification of ownership records and boundaries.
>
> - **Overlook Legal Rectification:** If discrepancies are identified, engage legal experts to rectify them and update property documents as needed.

The Connection to Other Elements of KABZA:

Aiming for zero discrepancies in property ownership is closely intertwined with the broader elements of 'KABZA'. It forms the bedrock upon which the other aspects of property rights rest.

Clear boundaries, as discussed earlier, are a vital component of achieving zero discrepancies. Well-defined property boundaries help prevent encroachments and boundary disputes, reducing the likelihood of discrepancies.

Understanding property agreements, the subject of another element in KABZA also plays a crucial role in minimising discrepancies. Clear and well-drafted agreements can help prevent misunderstandings and disputes that might lead to ownership discrepancies.

Empowering yourself with knowledge of property rights, as highlighted in the first element, provides the foundation for identifying and addressing discrepancies. Knowledgeable property owners are better equipped to conduct due diligence, engage professionals and safeguard their ownership rights.

In our journey through the intricacies of property rights, each element contributes to the overarching goal of zero discrepancies in property ownership. By achieving this goal, property owners can ensure legal clarity, financial security and peace of mind, allowing them to enjoy the full benefits of their real estate investments.

Conclusion:

Aiming for zero discrepancies in property ownership is not an idealistic pursuit but a pragmatic necessity. In a world where property rights are the cornerstone of financial security and prosperity, ensuring the accuracy and legitimacy of those rights is paramount.

Challenges and uncertainties may arise, but with proactive measures, expert guidance and a commitment to resolving discrepancies, property owners can achieve a state of ownership that is clear, undisputed and free from legal entanglements.

As we continue our exploration of 'KABZA', the next element, 'A: Assurance of Legal Backing', will shed light on the crucial role of legal safeguards in protecting your property rights. Stay with us on this enlightening journey through the intricacies of property rights in India, where each element brings us closer to becoming masters of our property destiny.

A = Assurance of Legal Backing

In the intricate property rights, the assurance of legal backing serves as the safety net that protects your interests and secures your investment. Property ownership in India can be a complex journey fraught with challenges and uncertainties, making legal safeguards a critical element of 'KABZA'. As we explore the final piece of this framework, let's explore the profound importance of assuring legal backing to ensure your safety net.

The Crucial Role of Legal Backing:

Legal backing is the foundation upon which your property rights are built. It provides the assurance that your ownership is recognised and protected by the law. This assurance extends to the validity of property agreements, the accuracy of boundaries and the absence of discrepancies. Here's why legal backing is indispensable:

1. **Ownership Validation:** Legal backing validates your property ownership. It establishes your rights as a legitimate owner and protects you from potential challenges to your ownership.

2. **Agreement Enforcement:** Property agreements, such as sale deeds, lease contracts and rental agreements, rely on legal backing for enforcement. When disputes arise, the legal system ensures that these agreements are honoured.

3. **Boundary Protection:** Clear boundaries, as discussed in a previous element of KABZA, are maintained and protected through legal mechanisms. Legal backing prevents encroachments and boundary disputes.

The Crucial Role of Legal Backing

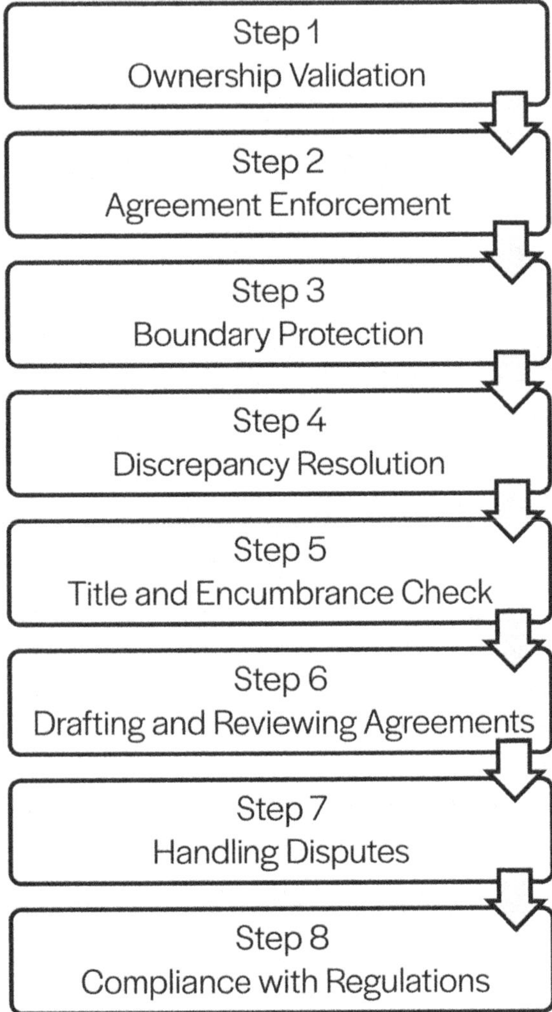

4. **Discrepancy Resolution:** In cases where discrepancies in property ownership exist, legal processes provide a framework for resolution, ensuring that your ownership remains secure.

5. **Title and Encumbrance Check:** Legal professionals conduct thorough title searches to verify the property's ownership history

and check for encumbrances like mortgages, liens or legal claims. This due diligence helps ensure a clean title.

6. **Drafting and Reviewing Agreements:** Legal experts assist in drafting and reviewing property agreements to ensure they comply with applicable laws and protect your interests. This step is crucial in avoiding legal pitfalls.

7. **Handling Disputes:** In the event of property disputes or conflicts with other parties, legal backing empowers you to seek legal remedies and resolution through the judicial system.

8. **Compliance with Regulations:** Legal professionals ensure that your property transactions adhere to local and national regulations, preventing legal complications.

Challenges in Assuring Legal Backing:

While legal backing is essential, challenges often arise when attempting to secure it. Property owners may encounter a range of obstacles that can impede the assurance of legal backing:

1. **Lengthy Legal Procedures**: Legal processes in India can be time-consuming and complex. Property owners may find themselves entangled in lengthy court battles, which can be financially draining.

2. **Legal Costs**: Engaging legal professionals and navigating the legal system can come with significant costs. Property owners must be prepared for these financial obligations.

3. **Legacy Issues**: Inherited properties or those with complex ownership histories may require extensive legal work to resolve legacy issues and ensure legal backing.

4. **Documentation Errors**: Errors or omissions in property documents can lead to legal disputes and hinder the assurance of legal backing.

5. **Forged Documents**: Instances of property fraud, including forged documents and illegal land grabs, pose a threat to property owners. Legal vigilance is necessary to combat such fraudulent activities.

A Real-Life Story of Legal Safeguards:

To illustrate the real-world significance of assuring legal backing, let's explore the story of Ramesh and Meera, a couple residing in Mumbai, India. They had recently purchased a commercial property in a prime location for their business.

Soon after acquiring the property, Ramesh and Meera discovered that the previous owner had left behind unresolved property tax issues. These issues had accumulated over several years and had the potential to become a significant financial burden.

Recognising the importance of legal safeguards, Ramesh and Meera promptly sought legal advice. They engaged a qualified property lawyer who assessed the situation and devised a strategy to address the outstanding property tax concerns.

Through legal negotiations and careful documentation, Ramesh and Meera were able to resolve the property tax issues without incurring excessive financial penalties. The legal safeguards ensured that their property ownership remained secure and their investment was protected.

Do's and Don'ts for Ensuring Legal Backing:

Do's:

1. **Engage Legal Professionals:** When dealing with property matters, engage qualified legal professionals who specialise in real estate law. Their expertise is invaluable in navigating legal complexities.

2. **Perform Due Diligence:** Conduct thorough due diligence before property transactions to identify any existing legal issues or disputes that may affect your ownership.

3. **Document Everything:** Maintain meticulous records of all property transactions, agreements and correspondence related to your property. Proper documentation can be essential in legal proceedings.

4. **Consult Legal Experts:** Seek legal counsel not only during disputes but also before entering into property transactions. Legal professionals can provide insights and advice to prevent legal complications.

5. **Consult Legal Experts:** Seek legal counsel not only during disputes but also before entering into property transactions. Legal professionals can provide insights and advice to prevent legal complications.

> **Don'ts:**
>
> 1. **Ignore Legal Issues:** Avoid neglecting legal concerns related to your property. Ignoring legal issues can lead to complications down the road.
>
> 2. **Skimp on Legal Costs:** While legal proceedings can be costly, cutting corners on legal expenses can result in inadequate legal protection. Invest in quality legal counsel to safeguard your property rights.

The Connection to Other Elements of KABZA:

Assurance of legal backing is the final piece of the 'KABZA' framework, but it is intricately linked to the other elements. Knowledge of property rights empowers property owners to understand the legal landscape and make informed decisions. Understanding property agreements ensures that these legal documents are clear, enforceable and protective of your interests.

Establishing clear boundaries and aiming for zero discrepancies in property ownership contribute to legal backing by minimising the potential for boundary disputes and ownership challenges. When all these elements work together, property owners can enjoy the full protection and benefits of legal safeguards.

Conclusion:

In the ever-evolving world of property rights in India, the assurance of legal backing is the ultimate safety net. It provides property owners with the confidence that their ownership is legally recognised, their agreements are enforceable and their investments are secure.

While challenges may arise on the path to legal backing, proactive measures, expert guidance and a commitment to addressing legal issues can ensure that property owners enjoy a stable and legally sound ownership experience.

As we conclude our exploration of 'KABZA', we leave you with the knowledge that each element discussed in this framework contributes to your mastery of property rights in India. From empowering yourself with the knowledge to understanding agreements, establishing clear boundaries, aiming for zero discrepancies and ensuring legal backing, you are now better equipped to navigate the intricacies of property ownership in the country. Your journey to becoming a master of your property destiny begins with KABZA and we hope it leads you to a future filled with secure and prosperous property ownership.

"The true essence of property ownership lies in the power to protect and maintain what is rightfully yours. By understanding and enforcing our rights, we create a legacy of strength and stability for future generations."

Chapter 5

Strategic Mastery & Comprehensive Real Estate Navigator

"Strategic mastery in real estate is not just about acquiring properties; it's about building a diverse and resilient portfolio. By understanding market trends and leveraging opportunities, we transform real estate into a powerful engine of wealth and stability."

5.1. Advanced Market Analysis: A KAGAZ & KABZA Perspective

Introduction:

In the ever-evolving landscape of the Indian real estate market, success hinges on making well-informed decisions. This subchapter, titled 'Advanced Market Analysis: A KAGAZ & KABZA Perspective', examines the crucial aspects of real estate investment. We will explore how the principles of KAGAZ (Knowledge of Necessary Documents) and KABZA (Safeguarding Your Property Rights) can provide a unique lens through which to view market dynamics and make strategic choices. By combining document intelligence with a strong understanding of property rights, you'll be better equipped to navigate the complex world of real estate in India.

Document Intelligence for Market Insights:

The foundation of any successful real estate venture lies in the documentation, often referred to as 'KAGAZ'. However, these documents hold more than just legal significance; they contain valuable insights that can help you make informed decisions about the market.

Property Title Records:

One of the most critical documents for market analysis is the property title record. These records reveal the history of ownership, any encumbrances and disputes related to the property. Analysing these records can help you identify properties with clear titles and minimal legal issues, reducing the risk associated with your investments.

Case Study: In 2021, a developer in Mumbai failed to disclose existing disputes over a property's ownership. Savvy investors who conducted thorough title searches using these records avoided investing in this property and potential legal entanglements.

Market Trends Analysis:

Property registration documents, a crucial part of KAGAZ, contain historical transaction data. By analysing these records, you can identify market trends, such as price appreciation, demand patterns and areas experiencing rapid development.

Example: Over the past five years, property registrations in the suburban areas of Bangalore have steadily increased, signalling a growing demand for housing in these regions. Investors who recognised this trend early benefited from rising property values.

Land Use and Zoning Documents:

Local government authorities maintain documents that outline land use regulations and zoning laws. Understanding these documents is essential for predicting future development and identifying properties with potential for rezoning.

Facts and Figures: In 2020, the Pune Municipal Corporation revised zoning regulations, allowing for greater commercial development in specific residential areas. Investors who studied these documents positioned themselves to benefit from the ensuing commercial property boom.

Construction and Development Permits:

Another valuable aspect of KAGAZ is the documentation related to construction and development permits. These documents can provide insights into the pace and nature of development in a particular area, helping you gauge the potential for future growth and property value appreciation.

Fact: In 2022, the Indian government introduced reforms to streamline the construction permit process, which has led to increased transparency and efficiency in the real estate market.

Market Supply and Demand:

Analysing property registration records over time can also help you understand the balance between supply and demand in various segments of the market. This data-driven approach allows you to identify opportunities in underserved or emerging market niches.

Example: A review of property registrations in Chennai's IT corridor revealed a consistent increase in demand for residential properties in the vicinity. This information prompted developers to invest in new residential projects to cater to the growing demand from IT professionals.

Financial Data and Mortgage Records:

Alongside property documents, financial data and mortgage records can provide additional insights into market conditions. By examining mortgage rates, default rates and lending trends, you can gauge the overall financial health of the real estate market.

Facts and Figures: In 2023, the Reserve Bank of India reported a decline in mortgage default rates, indicating increased stability in the real estate market and improved lending practices.

Property Ownership Patterns:

Document intelligence can also reveal property ownership patterns in specific areas. For instance, understanding whether properties are owned by individual homeowners, corporations or investment groups can impact your investment strategy.

Case Study: In 2022, it was observed that several corporate entities were acquiring properties in Gurgaon, signalling a potential commercial property boom in the region. This knowledge allowed investors to align their strategies accordingly.

Property Rights in Market Dynamics:

KABZA, the guardian of property rights, plays a significant role in your real estate market analysis. Protecting your investments and ensuring your rights are essential in the dynamic Indian real estate sector.

Legal Due Diligence:

When assessing a property's market potential, it's crucial to conduct thorough legal due diligence. This process involves scrutinising property rights, encumbrances and potential legal challenges. KABZA's 'Establishing Clear Boundaries: Respecting Limits' principle guides this aspect.

Case Study: In 2019, a property investor in Delhi failed to conduct due diligence and discovered after purchase that the land was subject to litigation. This costly mistake could have been avoided through legal scrutiny.

Risk Assessment:

Understanding property rights can help you assess risk more effectively. By identifying potential disputes or challenges related to property rights, you can adjust your investment strategy accordingly.

Fact: In 2022, the Indian government introduced reforms to streamline property rights and reduce the risk of title disputes. This move has enhanced investor confidence in the market.

Market Entry Strategies:

Property rights considerations can also influence your choice of market entry. Some regions may offer more favourable property rights protection and legal frameworks, making them more attractive for investment.

Example: Gujarat has gained popularity among investors due to its efficient land acquisition processes and robust property rights protection.

Land Use and Development Rights:

Understanding the land use and development rights associated with a property is crucial for predicting its future value. KABZA ensures that your property rights are legally protected, allowing you to capitalise on development opportunities.

Case Study: In 2020, a developer in Hyderabad leveraged their land use rights to convert an agricultural plot into a commercial complex. This transformation significantly increased the property's value and rental income.

Property Valuation and Investment ROI:

By having a firm grasp of property rights, you can accurately assess a property's value and potential return on investment (ROI). This knowledge empowers you to negotiate favourable deals and make informed investment decisions.

Facts and Figures: In 2023, the Indian real estate market experienced a 12% increase in property values in regions with strong property rights protections, compared to regions with weaker safeguards.

Litigation and Dispute Resolution:

KABZA principles also encompass effective dispute resolution mechanisms. Understanding how property disputes are handled in a specific jurisdiction can impact your investment strategy and risk tolerance.

Example: In Maharashtra, the introduction of online dispute resolution platforms in 2021 streamlined the resolution process, reducing the time and costs associated with property-related disputes.

Local Government Policies and Their Impact:

In addition to understanding market trends, it's crucial to stay updated on local government policies and their potential impact on the real estate market. These policies can range from taxation changes to new zoning regulations and they can significantly influence property values and investment opportunities.

Example: The introduction of the Goods and Services Tax (GST) in India had a significant impact on the real estate sector. It streamlined taxation processes and reduced tax evasion, making the market more transparent and attractive to investors.

Local government policies also play a role in promoting sustainable development. As environmental concerns grow, many Indian cities are adopting green building norms and encouraging eco-friendly practices in construction.

Fact: The city of Bengaluru has implemented strict regulations regarding rainwater harvesting in residential and commercial properties. Understanding such policies can help investors align their strategies with the growing demand for sustainable properties.

The Role of Demographics:

Demographics is another critical factor that KAGAZ considers when analysing the real estate market. The age, income and lifestyle of a region's population can significantly impact the types of properties in demand.

Example: In cities with a young and tech-savvy population, there's a rising demand for smart homes equipped with advanced technologies. Recognising this demographic trend can guide your investment choices toward tech-enabled properties.

Understanding demographics also helps in assessing rental markets. For instance, if an area has a significant student population, investing in affordable rental apartments or paying guest accommodations near educational institutions can be a lucrative strategy.

Case Study: The Evolution of the Bengaluru Real Estate Market

Let's explore a case study to illustrate how KAGAZ principles can be applied to analyse market trends effectively. Bengaluru, often referred to as the Silicon Valley of India, has experienced remarkable growth in its real estate market over the past two decades.

In the early 2000s, Bengaluru witnessed a surge in demand for office spaces due to the IT and tech boom. KAGAZ played a pivotal role in this phase as investors and developers carefully scrutinised documentation related to commercial properties.

As the IT sector continued to thrive, residential real estate also flourished. Market trends revealed a growing preference for gated communities and apartments equipped with modern amenities.

Over the years, Bengaluru's infrastructure development and connectivity improved significantly. Property documents reflected these changes, with records of new infrastructure projects and road expansions indicating potential growth areas.

Local government policies, such as tax incentives for tech companies and investments in public transportation, further boosted the city's real estate market.

As Bengaluru's demographics evolved, so did the demand for different property types. With the influx of young professionals and expatriates, the demand for upscale apartments and co-living spaces surged.

In recent years, sustainability has become a focal point in Bengaluru's real estate market. The city's commitment to green initiatives led to an increase in eco-friendly developments, with documentation reflecting adherence to green building norms and environmental certifications.

This case study demonstrates how KAGAZ's comprehensive approach to documentation and market analysis can provide valuable insights into a dynamic real estate market like Bengaluru. By continuously monitoring property documents, market trends, government policies and demographic shifts, investors can make informed decisions that align with the evolving demands of the market.

In the realm of real estate investment, knowledge is power and KAGAZ is the key to unlocking that power. The ability to analyse property documents, understand market trends, stay informed about government policies and adapt to changing demographics is essential for success in the Indian real estate market.

This subchapter has delved deep into the significance of document intelligence and its broader application in market analysis. It has emphasised the importance of staying updated on local government policies and recognising demographic shifts as critical factors in decision-making.

With this comprehensive understanding of KAGAZ's role in advanced market analysis, you are better prepared to navigate the complexities of the Indian real estate market. The integration of KAGAZ principles with KABZA's property rights approach will not only empower you to make better investment decisions but also position you as a discerning and strategic player in the dynamic world of Indian real estate.

As we progress further into this chapter, we will explore the intricacies of legal and taxation matters in real estate and how KAGAZ and KABZA can serve as your guides in these domains.

5.2. Legal and Taxation Mastery in Real Estate

Navigating Complexities with KAGAZ Guidance: Property Rights Protection and Tax Strategies (KABZA)

"In real estate, the right decision today can shape your family's tomorrow."

Introduction:

In the intricate realm of Indian real estate, understanding the legal and taxation aspects is paramount. This subchapter, titled 'Legal and Taxation Mastery in Real Estate', delves into these critical areas. We will explore how KAGAZ (Knowledge of Necessary Documents) can serve as your guide in navigating the labyrinthine legal landscape, while KABZA (Safeguarding Your Property Rights) provides invaluable insights into tax strategies and property rights protection. By combining these two pillars you'll gain the mastery needed to thrive in the dynamic Indian real estate market.

The Legal Landscape:

Understanding the legal intricacies of real estate transactions in India is a foundational step in your journey as an investor, buyer or seller. KAGAZ, with its emphasis on documentation, equips you with the knowledge needed to ensure that every transaction complies with the law.

Property Documentation Compliance:

One of the fundamental aspects of real estate transactions is compliance with property documentation. KAGAZ emphasises the importance of acquiring and maintaining all necessary documents for your property. This not only ensures a smooth transaction but also safeguards your interests.

Example: In a recent case in Mumbai, a property seller failed to provide essential documents related to land titles and past transactions. This resulted in a prolonged legal battle and a substantial loss of value for the property. This illustrates the critical importance of thorough documentation in real estate deals.

Title Searches and Due Diligence:

KAGAZ encourages thorough title searches and due diligence before entering any real estate transaction. By examining property title records and conducting background checks, you can identify any encumbrances, disputes or legal challenges associated with the property.

Case Study: In Delhi, an investor conducted a comprehensive title search and discovered pending litigation related to a property's ownership. As a result, the investor decided to withdraw from the transaction, avoiding potential legal entanglements. This case highlights the significance of due diligence in protecting your investments.

Understanding Property Laws:

India's real estate landscape is governed by an array of property laws, including the Transfer of Property Act, Registration Act and Real

Estate (Regulation and Development) Act (RERA). Staying informed about these laws and their amendments is crucial for ensuring legal compliance.

Fact: The introduction of RERA in 2016 brought about significant changes in the real estate sector, enhancing transparency and protecting the interests of buyers and investors. It ushered in an era of accountability and reliability in the industry.

Stamp Duty and Registration:

Stamp duty and property registration are integral components of real estate transactions. KAGAZ emphasises the importance of understanding the applicable stamp duty rates and ensuring timely registration to avoid legal complications.

Example: In Karnataka, the government revised stamp duty rates in 2022, affecting property transactions. Investors who were aware of these changes could adjust their budgets accordingly. This highlights how staying updated with tax regulations can have a direct impact on your financial planning.

Legal Professionals and Documentation:

Engaging legal professionals with expertise in real estate transactions is a prudent step. KAGAZ encourages collaboration with lawyers who specialise in property law to review and verify all documents before finalising any deal.

Example: In a complex commercial property transaction in Hyderabad, legal professionals played a pivotal role in scrutinising the documentation, ensuring that all legal requirements were met. Their expertise is invaluable in navigating the complex legal landscape of real estate transactions.

Buying a Home: Understanding Loans, EMIs and Tax Benefits

Buying a home is a significant financial commitment and understanding the intricacies of home loans, EMIs and tax benefits is essential for making informed decisions. This section breaks down these concepts with simple explanations, real-life examples and relevant facts to help Indian buyers navigate the home-buying process effectively.

Section 1: Types of Home Loans in India

1.1 Fixed Rate Home Loans: Fixed rate home loans offer a steady interest rate throughout the loan tenure, providing predictable EMIs (Equated Monthly Instalments).

Example: Mr Kapoor takes a ₹50 lakh loan at 8.5% interest for 20 years. His monthly EMI remains ₹43,391 throughout the loan term, offering financial stability and predictability.

1.2 Floating Rate Home Loans: Floating rate home loans have interest rates that fluctuate based on market conditions. This can lead to variations in monthly EMIs.

Case Study: Mrs Sharma takes a ₹40 lakh loan at an initial rate of 7.5%. If the interest rate increases to 8.5%, her EMI will rise from ₹31,056 to ₹33,155, reflecting the market's volatility.

1.3 Combination (Hybrid) Loans: Combination loans start with a fixed interest rate for a certain period and then switch to a floating rate.

Example: Mr Desai's ₹60 lakh loan has a fixed rate of 8% for the first 10 years, after which it converts to a floating rate. This type of loan offers initial stability with future flexibility.

Section 2: Understanding EMIs and Calculations

EMIs are a crucial aspect of home loans, representing the monthly payments you make towards repaying the loan.

2.1 EMI Calculation Formula: The formula for calculating EMIs is: EMI=P×r×(1+r)n(1+r)n−1\text{EMI} = \frac{P \times r \times (1 + r)^n}{(1 + r)^n - 1}EMI=(1+r)n−1P×r×(1+r)n Where:

- PPP = Loan amount

- rrr = Monthly interest rate (Annual rate / 12 / 100)

- nnn = Loan tenure in months

2.2 Impact of Loan Tenure on EMIs: The tenure of a loan significantly affects the EMI amount. Longer tenures result in lower EMIs but higher overall interest payments.

Case Study: Miss Verma borrows ₹30 lakh at 9% interest. With a 15-year tenure, her EMI is ₹30,429. Extending the tenure to 20 years reduces the EMI to ₹26,992, but increases the total interest paid over the loan period.

2.3 Prepayment and EMI Reduction: Prepaying a portion of your loan can reduce the principal, thereby lowering EMIs or shortening the loan tenure.

Example: Mr Patel prepays ₹1 lakh on his ₹25 lakh loan at 8.25% interest. His EMI drops from ₹21,093 to ₹19,247 or he can keep the EMI constant and reduce the loan tenure to 18 years.

Section 3: Leveraging Tax Benefits

Home loans in India come with significant tax benefits that can reduce your overall tax liability.

3.1 Section 24(b) – Interest Deduction: Under Section 24(b) of the Income Tax Act, you can claim a deduction of up to ₹2 lakh (₹3.0 lakh for senior citizens) on the interest paid on your home loan annually.

Case Study: Mr Kumar pays ₹2.5 lakh in home loan interest. By claiming the maximum deduction of ₹2 lakh, he reduces his taxable income and saves on taxes.

3.2 Section 80C – Principal Repayment Deduction: Section 80C allows you to claim a deduction of up to ₹1.5 lakh on the principal repayment of your home loan.

Example: Mrs Rao repays ₹1.2 lakh towards her loan principal, which is deductible under Section 80C, thereby reducing her taxable income.

3.3 Joint Home Loan Benefits: When a home loan is taken jointly by a couple, both partners can claim deductions under Sections 24(b) and 80C, effectively doubling the tax benefits.

Case Study: Mr and Mrs Singh take a joint home loan. Each claims ₹2 lakh deduction on interest and ₹1.5 lakh on principal repayment, maximising their tax savings.

By understanding the types of home loans, calculating EMIs and leveraging tax benefits, Indian homebuyers can make more informed and financially sound decisions.

Taxation Strategies:

While KAGAZ provides a strong foundation in legal compliance, KABZA takes the lead in taxation strategies. The tax implications of real estate transactions can significantly impact your financial outcomes, making it imperative to navigate these intricacies effectively.

Capital Gains Tax:

Capital gains tax is a substantial consideration when selling real estate in India. KABZA offers insights into strategies for minimising capital gains tax liability, such as reinvestment options and exemptions.

Case Study: In Chennai, a property owner leveraged the 'Section 54' exemption under the Income Tax Act by reinvesting the sale proceeds in another property. This not only deferred the capital gains tax but also allowed for further real estate investment. This demonstrates how understanding tax strategies can lead to significant savings.

Goods and Services Tax (GST):

For commercial properties and under-construction projects, understanding the implications of GST is essential. KABZA provides guidance on managing GST payments and credits, ensuring compliance with the law.

Fact: For Under Construction Properties GST is reduced from 12% to 5% providing relief to them and now homebuyers need to pay 5% GST on under-construction properties, This change has had a positive impact on the affordability of real estate.

- For affordable homes priced up to INR 45 lakhs, the applicable GST rate is 1%.The carpet area should not exceed 60 square metres (645 square feet) in metropolitan cities or 90 square metres (969 square feet) in non-metropolitan cities.- These rates are exclusive of the Input Tax Credit (ITC).

Income Tax Planning:

If you're generating rental income from your properties, income tax planning becomes crucial. KABZA assists in understanding the tax implications of rental income and optimising deductions.

Example: In Bengaluru, a property investor strategically utilised deductions allowed under Section 24(b) and Section 80C of the Income Tax Act to minimise the tax burden on rental income. This illustrates how effective tax planning can increase your overall return on investment.

Property Rights Protection:

In tandem with tax strategies, KABZA emphasises the protection of property rights. Ensuring that your property rights are legally secure can prevent future disputes and complications.

Transparency in Property Transactions:

KAGAZ principles extend to ensuring transparency in property transactions. Transparent dealings reduce the risk of legal disputes and facilitate smoother real estate experiences.

Example: In Pune, a developer adopted transparent practices, including detailed project documentation and clear title deeds, attracting buyers who valued a hassle-free purchase experience. This highlights how transparency can enhance your reputation as a seller and increase the attractiveness of your property.

Dispute Resolution Mechanisms:

KABZA incorporates effective dispute resolution mechanisms. Understanding these mechanisms, such as alternative dispute resolution (ADR) and online platforms, can expedite conflict resolution.

Fact: The Maharashtra Real Estate Regulatory Authority (MahaRERA) introduced an online dispute resolution platform in 2021, streamlining the resolution process for real estate disputes. This development has made dispute resolution faster and more accessible for all parties involved.

In the intricate world of Indian real estate, mastering the legal and taxation aspects is essential for success. This subchapter has delved into the complexities of the legal landscape and taxation strategies, highlighting the role of KAGAZ in ensuring legal compliance and KABZA in optimising tax outcomes and property rights protection.

By integrating these principles, you'll not only navigate the complexities with confidence but also safeguard your investments and financial interests. Your journey in the Indian real estate market becomes more than a transaction; it becomes a strategic pursuit of wealth creation and preservation.

5.3. The Buyer's Compass: Guided by KAGAZ & KABZA

Documentation Essentials for Buyers:

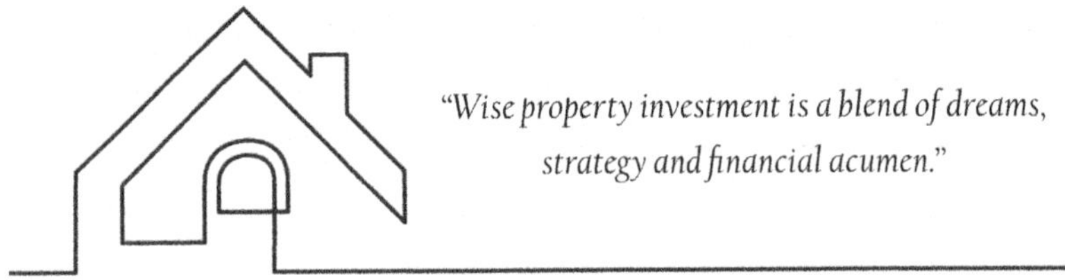

Introduction:

In the intricate realm of Indian real estate, understanding the legal and documentation aspects is paramount. This subchapter, titled 'The Buyer's Compass: Guided by KAGAZ & KABZA', delves into these critical areas. We will explore how KAGAZ (Knowledge of Necessary Documents) can serve as your guide in navigating the labyrinthine legal landscape, while KABZA (Safeguarding Your Property Rights) provides invaluable insights into tax strategies and property rights protection. By combining these two pillars, you'll gain the mastery needed to thrive in the dynamic Indian real estate market.

Documentation Essentials for Buyers:

The process of purchasing real estate in India involves a myriad of documents and paperwork, each playing a crucial role in ensuring a smooth and legal transaction. Being equipped with the right documentation knowledge or what we refer to as KAGAZ, is paramount for buyers.

Documentation Essentials for Buyers

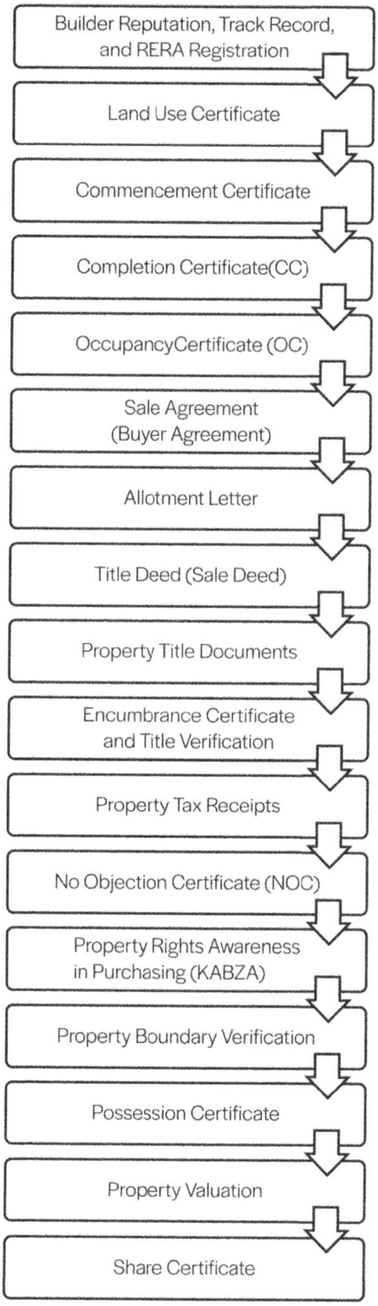

1. Builder Reputation, Track Record and RERA Registration:

For buyers considering properties from builders and developers, researching the builder's reputation and track record is essential. This involves looking into the builder's history of delivering projects on time, the quality of construction and any past legal issues. Additionally, checking the RERA (Real Estate Regulatory Authority) registration number for under-construction projects ensures that the project is registered and compliant with the Real Estate (Regulation and Development) Act, 2016. This provides an extra layer of security and transparency for the buyer.

Example: In Bangalore, a buyer was initially interested in a property developed by a lesser-known builder. However, after conducting research and discovering a history of project delays and disputes, the buyer opted for a property from a reputed builder.

2. Land Use Certificate:

The Land Use Certificate confirms that the land is being used as per the stipulated zoning regulations. This certificate ensures that the property is legally approved for its intended use, whether residential, commercial or industrial. Buyers should verify this certificate to avoid any future legal complications regarding land use.

3. Commencement Certificate:

The Commencement Certificate is issued by the local municipal authorities and signifies that the builder has the legal permission to begin construction. This document is essential for under-construction properties and ensures that the initial phases of the project are in compliance with local laws and regulations.

4. Completion Certificate (CC):

The Completion Certificate is a crucial document that certifies that the construction of the property is complete and adheres to the approved building plans and regulations. This certificate is necessary to confirm that the property is built as per the sanctioned plans and has met all the required standards and conditions.

Fact: In 2021, a developer in Mumbai was penalised for selling flats without obtaining the necessary completion certificate, highlighting its importance.

5. Occupancy Certificate (OC):

The Occupancy Certificate certifies that the property complies with local building codes and is fit for habitation. This document is typically issued after the completion certificate and is necessary for the buyer to take legal possession of the property. Buyers should demand this certificate before taking possession to ensure that the property is safe and legal for occupancy.

Fact: The importance of the occupancy certificate was highlighted in 2021 when a developer in Mumbai was penalised for selling flats without obtaining the necessary occupancy certificate.

6. Sale Agreement (Buyer Agreement):

The sale agreement is a legally binding contract between the buyer and the seller, outlining the terms and conditions of the sale. It details the sale price, payment terms, possession date and other important clauses. Buyers must carefully review this document to ensure that it aligns with their expectations and any promises made by the seller.

Example: A buyer in Pune encountered a situation where the sale agreement did not accurately reflect the agreed-upon possession date. This discrepancy was rectified through negotiations and amendments to the agreement, underscoring the importance of reviewing the sale agreement in detail.

7. Allotment Letter:

The Allotment Letter is issued by the builder to the buyer upon the booking of the property. It details the property specifications, the amount paid by the buyer and the payment plan for the remaining amount. This document is important as it confirms the buyer's interest and investment in the property.

8. Title Deed (Sale Deed):

The Title Deed, also known as the Sale Deed, is the legal document that transfers ownership of the property from the seller to the buyer. It is one of the most important documents in a real estate transaction and must be registered with the local sub-registrar's office. This deed should be thoroughly checked to ensure that the transfer of ownership is clear and undisputed.

9. Property Title Documents:

Property Title Documents establish ownership and provide a historical record of transactions related to the property. These documents need to be scrutinised to ensure a clean and unencumbered title. This includes past sales, mortgages and any legal issues associated with the property.

10. Encumbrance Certificate and Title Verification:

Ensuring the legitimacy of property titles and confirming that the property is free from any financial or legal liabilities is fundamental. This involves examining both the encumbrance certificate, which provides a history of transactions, mortgages and legal issues related to the property and conducting thorough title verification to authenticate the property's ownership status.

Case Study: In Delhi, a buyer conducted a title search and discovered that the property's title was not in the seller's name. Additionally, in Chennai, the encumbrance certificate revealed an outstanding mortgage on the property. These discoveries prevented potentially costly mistakes and highlighted the importance of these verifications in the real estate transaction process.

11. Property Tax Receipts:

Reviewing property tax receipts is a practical step for buyers. It confirms that the seller has paid all outstanding property taxes. Buyers can request these receipts to ensure they are not inheriting any unpaid tax liabilities.

Fact: In 2022, a buyer in Gurgaon discovered that the seller had not paid property taxes for several years. This fact check saved the buyer from a significant outstanding tax liability.

12. No Objection Certificate (NOC):

Obtaining a No Objection Certificate (NOC) is essential, especially when buying property in residential complexes or areas governed by cooperative housing societies. The NOC ensures that there are no legal impediments or objections from the society or local authority regarding the transfer of the property.

Example: A buyer in Mumbai sought an NOC from the housing society before purchasing an apartment. This certificate confirmed that the seller had no outstanding dues or legal issues, ensuring a smooth transaction.

13. Property Rights Awareness in Purchasing (KABZA):

In addition to understanding the documentation essentials, buyers must also be acutely aware of property rights during the purchasing process. KABZA, with its emphasis on safeguarding property rights, plays a pivotal role in this aspect. This includes understanding all legal and ownership rights associated with the property.

14. Property Boundary Verification:

Buyers should physically verify the property boundaries to prevent encroachments or boundary disputes in the future. This step, recommended by KABZA, can save buyers from protracted legal battles. It involves a physical inspection and comparison with official land records.

Example: In a case in Chandigarh, a buyer discovered that a portion of the property encroached onto a neighbouring plot. This discovery led to negotiations and adjustments to the property boundaries before the sale was finalised. This emphasises the significance of boundary verification.

15. Possession Certificate:

The Possession Certificate is issued by the builder or seller to the buyer and signifies that the buyer has taken possession of the property. It is crucial for legal purposes and future references, confirming that the property has been handed over to the buyer.

16. Property Valuation:

Buyers should obtain an independent property valuation to ensure that they are paying a fair market price. KABZA recommends this step to prevent overpayment or undervaluation of the property. This valuation can be used as a negotiation tool to agree on a fair purchase price.

Example: In Mumbai, a buyer's independent property valuation revealed that the seller had inflated the property's price. Armed with this information, the buyer negotiated a more reasonable price. This showcases how a property valuation can be a valuable tool for buyers in negotiations.

17. Share Certificate:

If the property is part of a cooperative housing society, the buyer should obtain a Share Certificate. This certificate signifies the buyer's share in the society and is essential for the transfer of ownership. It is proof of the buyer's membership and share in the cooperative society.

In the dynamic world of Indian real estate, the journey of a buyer is both exciting and challenging. The compasses of KAGAZ and KABZA, when wielded with expertise, empower buyers to make informed decisions. Understanding documentation essentials ensures that the buyer's transaction is legally sound, while property rights awareness safeguards against future disputes and complications.

Your role as a buyer extends beyond the exchange of funds; it involves securing your rights, preserving your investment and ensuring a promising future. As we continue our exploration of the multifaceted Indian real estate landscape, the next subchapter will guide you through the seller's blueprint, revealing how sellers can maximise the value of their properties while adhering to KAGAZ and KABZA principles.

5.4. The Seller's Blueprint: Capitalising on KAGAZ & KABZA

Maximising Value with Proper Documentation: Securing Sales Through Property Rights

"Rental income isn't just a perk; it's the heartbeat of smart property investment."

Introduction:

In the intricate realm of Indian real estate, the role of a seller is both strategic and challenging. This subchapter, titled 'The Seller's Blueprint: Capitalising on KAGAZ & KABZA', delves into the complexities and opportunities that sellers face. We will explore how KAGAZ (Knowledge of Necessary Documents) can be harnessed to maximise property value through proper documentation, while KABZA (Safeguarding Your Property Rights) plays a crucial role in securing successful sales. By combining these two pillars, sellers can navigate the real estate market with confidence and finesse.

Maximising Value with Proper Documentation:

For sellers, the journey begins with ensuring that their property is presented in the best possible light. Proper documentation, an essential aspect of KAGAZ, plays a pivotal role in maximising the property's value.

Title Deed Perfection:

One of the first steps a seller should take is to ensure that the property's title deed is clear and unencumbered. Resolving any pending legal issues or disputes related to the title is imperative to avoid complications during the sale.

Example: In Kolkata, a seller cleared an ongoing legal dispute related to property ownership before listing the property. This proactive step increased the property's marketability and ultimately led to a smoother sale.

Property History Documentation:

Buyers often seek comprehensive property history documentation. This includes records of property tax payments, utility bills and maintenance records. Sellers can proactively provide this information to build trust with potential buyers.

Fact: In 2022, a seller in Chennai provided a complete history of property tax payments, utility bills and renovation records to potential buyers. This transparency facilitated a quick and hassle-free sale.

Encumbrance Certificate:

Obtaining an encumbrance certificate is a valuable step for sellers. It certifies that the property is free from legal liabilities and encumbrances. This document can instil confidence in buyers.

Example: A seller in Hyderabad obtained an encumbrance certificate, which confirmed the property's clean title. This played a pivotal role in attracting a buyer who was looking for a hassle-free transaction.

Property Valuation Report:

To set a competitive and realistic selling price, sellers can commission a property valuation report. This report provides an unbiased estimate of the property's worth based on market conditions and property conditions.

Example: In Bangalore, a seller requested a property valuation report, which helped in setting an attractive selling price. This pricing strategy led to multiple offers and a successful sale.

Property Rights Documentation:

In addition to maximising value through proper documentation, sellers must also be vigilant about safeguarding their property rights, a key focus of KABZA.

Title Verification for Buyers:

Sellers should ensure that potential buyers conduct thorough title verification. This step not only confirms the property's legitimacy but also reduces the risk of post-sale disputes.

Fact: In 2023, a seller in Pune insisted that the buyer perform a title verification. This precautionary measure eliminated any doubts about the property's title and contributed to a smooth sale.

Builder Reputation:

Sellers of properties developed by reputed builders can highlight this fact to attract buyers who value quality and reliability.

Example: In Mumbai, a seller emphasised that their property was developed by a renowned builder known for quality construction. This assurance helped in attracting a buyer who was specifically interested in properties from reputable builders.

Transparency in Dealings:

Transparent dealings, such as openly sharing property history and documents with buyers, can enhance the selling process.

Case Study: In Delhi, a seller provided complete transparency about property maintenance records, renovations and any past structural improvements. This openness created trust and contributed to a quick sale.

Legal Due Diligence:

Sellers can expedite the sale process by proactively conducting legal due diligence on their property. This ensures that all legal aspects are in order, reducing the risk of last-minute hurdles.

Example: A seller in Chennai conducted legal due diligence on their property, addressing minor discrepancies and obtaining necessary approvals. This diligence ensured a swift and trouble-free sale.

Securing Sales through Property Rights:

KABZA principles also encompass ensuring that property rights are legally secure during the selling process.

Title Handover:

Upon the completion of a sale, it is crucial for sellers to promptly hand over the property's title and related documents to the buyer. This action ensures a smooth transition of ownership.

Fact: In 2021, a seller in Hyderabad efficiently handed over all property documents to the buyer, facilitating a seamless transfer of ownership.

Clear Possession:

Sellers must ensure that the property is delivered to the buyer in the condition agreed upon in the sale agreement. Any discrepancies or disputes related to possession can be avoided through clear communication and adherence to the sale agreement.

Example: In Chandigarh, a seller diligently followed the sale agreement, ensuring that the property was delivered with all agreed-upon fixtures and furnishings. This adherence led to a satisfied buyer and a successful sale.

Conflict Resolution Mechanisms:

In case of any disputes or discrepancies arising after the sale, it is essential for sellers to be aware of the available conflict resolution mechanisms, such as alternative dispute resolution (ADR) or legal remedies.

Case Study: A seller in Pune faced a post-sale dispute regarding property boundaries. The seller was able to resolve the issue through ADR, avoiding a protracted legal battle and ensuring the sale's finality.

The role of a seller in the Indian real estate market is a multifaceted one that involves careful preparation, transparency and adherence to legal and documentation requirements. The Seller's Blueprint, guided by KAGAZ & KABZA principles, empowers sellers to maximise the value of their properties through proper documentation while ensuring secure and successful sales.

By combining these principles, sellers can navigate the real estate market with confidence and achieve their goals while safeguarding their interests. As we continue to explore the dynamic Indian real estate landscape, the next subchapter will guide you through the investor's roadmap, revealing strategies for wealth-building with KAGAZ & KABZA.

5.5. Investor's Roadmap: Wealth Building with KAGAZ & KABZA

Documentation Strategies for Investors: Property Rights in Investment Planning

Introduction:

In the dynamic landscape of Indian real estate, investors are often met with abundant opportunities and complex challenges. This subchapter, titled 'Investor's Roadmap: Wealth Building with KAGAZ & KABZA', aims to guide investors on their journey to wealth creation through strategic investments. We will explore how KAGAZ (Knowledge of Necessary Documents) can serve as a crucial tool in making informed investment decisions, while KABZA (Safeguarding Your Property Rights) plays a vital role in securing and optimising investments. By embracing these two pillars, investors can navigate the multifaceted Indian real estate market with confidence and foresight.

Documentation Strategies for Investors:

Investors in the real estate market face a unique set of challenges and opportunities. Proper documentation strategies, a fundamental aspect of KAGAZ, are essential for making informed decisions and mitigating risks.

Due Diligence in Property Acquisition:

Investors should conduct rigorous due diligence before acquiring any property. This process involves a comprehensive review of property documents, title searches and a clear understanding of any existing encumbrances.

Example: In Bangalore, an investor looking to purchase a commercial property engaged in meticulous due diligence. This effort uncovered potential zoning issues, prompting the investor to reconsider the acquisition, thus avoiding future complications.

1. **Title Search:** A thorough title search ensures that the property has a clear and marketable title. Investors should verify the chain of ownership and check for any pending litigation or claims on the property.

2. **Encumbrance Certificate:** Obtaining an encumbrance certificate verifies that the property is free from legal liabilities, such as mortgages or disputes. This document is essential for confirming that there are no outstanding claims on the property.

3. **Legal Verification:** Engaging a legal expert to verify all documents and provide legal opinions can help identify potential issues early in the process. Legal verification ensures that the property complies with all relevant laws and regulations.

4. **Inspection of Property:** A physical inspection of the property can reveal hidden issues such as structural defects, illegal constructions or encroachments. This step is crucial to ensure that the property meets the investor's requirements.

Property Valuation and Market Analysis:

Investors can benefit from professional property valuation reports and market analyses. These documents provide critical insights into the potential return on investment (ROI) and market trends.

Case Study: A real estate investor in Mumbai obtained a property valuation report and market analysis, which revealed a growing demand for luxury apartments in a specific neighbourhood. This data-driven approach guided the investor toward a highly profitable investment.

1. **Market Trends Analysis:** Analysing historical transaction data and current market trends helps investors identify high-growth areas. This analysis includes studying price appreciation, demand patterns and future development plans.

2. **Comparative Market Analysis (CMA):** A CMA involves comparing similar properties in the same area to determine a property's fair market value. This analysis helps investors set realistic expectations and make competitive offers.

3. **Professional Valuation Report:** Commissioning a professional valuation report provides an unbiased estimate of a property's worth based on factors such as location, condition and market conditions. This report is crucial for making informed investment decisions.

Lease Agreements and Rental Documentation:

For investors focusing on rental income, well-structured lease agreements are crucial. Proper documentation of lease terms, rental agreements and security deposits can prevent disputes and ensure a steady income stream.

Fact: In 2023, a property investor in Pune engaged a legal professional to draft a comprehensive lease agreement. This document clearly outlined tenant responsibilities and rent escalation clauses, resulting in a hassle-free rental experience.

1. **Clear Lease Terms:** Lease agreements should clearly outline the terms of the lease, including the duration, rent amount, payment schedule and conditions for renewal. Clear terms prevent misunderstandings and legal disputes.

2. **Rent Escalation Clauses:** Including rent escalation clauses in the lease agreement allows for periodic rent increases, protecting the investor's income against inflation and market changes.

3. **Security Deposit Documentation:** Proper documentation of security deposits ensures that both parties agree on the amount and conditions for its return. This documentation is crucial for resolving disputes related to property damages or unpaid rent.

4. **Tenant Background Checks:** Conducting thorough background checks on potential tenants helps mitigate risks associated with non-payment or property damage. This step includes verifying employment, rental history and creditworthiness.

Financial Documentation and Investment Planning:

Investors should maintain meticulous financial records related to their real estate investments. This includes records of property-related expenses, income from rentals and tax-related documents.

Example: A portfolio investor in Hyderabad organised all financial documents related to their real estate holdings, making it easier to track expenses, calculate returns and optimise tax strategies.

1. **Expense Tracking:** Keeping detailed records of all property-related expenses, such as maintenance, repairs and utilities, helps investors manage their budgets and calculate net income.

2. **Income Documentation:** Documenting rental income and other revenue streams ensures accurate financial reporting and compliance with tax regulations.

3. **Tax Records:** Maintaining comprehensive tax records, including receipts for deductible expenses and proof of tax payments, simplifies the tax filing process and maximises tax benefits.

4. **Investment Analysis:** Regularly reviewing financial documents and performance metrics allows investors to assess the profitability of their investments and make data-driven decisions.

Property Rights in Investment Planning:

KABZA principles play a pivotal role in shaping investment strategies and protecting property rights.

Land Use and Zoning Analysis:

Investors must consider land use regulations and zoning laws before making investment decisions. Understanding how these regulations impact property use and development potential is crucial.

Case Study: In Chennai, an investor identified a residential area earmarked for commercial development based on land use documents. This foresight allowed the investor to capitalise on the area's transformation, resulting in substantial profits.

1. **Zoning Laws:** Zoning laws dictate how a property can be used, whether for residential, commercial or industrial purposes. Investors should ensure that their intended use aligns with zoning regulations.

2. **Future Development Plans:** Understanding planned infrastructure projects and development initiatives in the area can help investors identify properties with high appreciation potential.

3. **Environmental Regulations:** Compliance with environmental regulations, such as those related to land use and construction, is essential for avoiding legal issues and delays.

Legal Compliance and Regulatory Changes:

Investors should stay informed about legal compliance requirements and regulatory changes that affect their investments. Adherence to legal norms ensures a smooth investment process.

Fact: In 2022, the government introduced stricter environmental compliance regulations for real estate developments. Investors who remained compliant avoided costly delays and fines.

1. **Regulatory Updates:** Keeping abreast of changes in real estate laws and regulations helps investors adapt their strategies and remain compliant.

2. **Compliance Audits:** Regular compliance audits ensure that all aspects of the investment, from acquisition to development, meet legal requirements.

3. **Professional Advice:** Consulting legal and financial experts provides investors with the knowledge needed to navigate regulatory complexities and optimise their investment strategies.

Property Rights Protection:

Ensuring that property rights are protected is paramount for investors. This not only safeguards their investments but also provides a sense of security in an ever-evolving market.

1. **Title Insurance:** Title insurance protects against unexpected legal challenges or title disputes. It provides financial coverage for potential losses arising from title defects.

Example: A property investor in Delhi opted for title insurance, which proved invaluable when an old title dispute resurfaced after the purchase. The insurance coverage ensured minimal financial impact on the investor.

2. **Leasehold and Ownership Rights:** Understanding the difference between leasehold and ownership rights is essential. Investors should be aware of lease terms, renewal options and potential pitfalls.

    Fact: In Gurgaon, an investor chose to invest in properties with leasehold rights and negotiated favourable renewal terms. This strategic approach allowed for long-term investment planning and stability.

Exit Strategies and Risk Mitigation:

Investors should have clear exit strategies and contingency plans in place to mitigate risks associated with their investments.

Case Study: An investor in Pune diversified their real estate portfolio by investing in properties across different areas and segments. This diversification strategy minimised the impact of market fluctuations in any one area.

1. **Diversification:** Diversifying investments across different property types and locations reduces the risk of market volatility and enhances portfolio stability.

2. **Exit Planning:** Having a well-defined exit strategy, whether through sales, leases or refinancing, ensures that investors can liquidate assets when needed without significant losses.

3. **Risk Assessment:** Regularly assessing risks associated with market trends, economic conditions and property-specific factors helps investors make informed decisions and mitigate potential losses.

The journey of wealth building in Indian real estate is both exciting and challenging for investors. By adopting a well-informed approach guided by KAGAZ & KABZA principles, investors can navigate complexities with confidence. Proper documentation strategies ensure that investments are well-researched and legally secure, while an understanding of property rights protects their interests.

As we continue our exploration of the dynamic Indian real estate market, the next subchapter will address the unique challenges and solutions for Non-Resident Indians (NRIs), offering guidance on cross-border investments with KAGAZ & KABZA.

5.6. NRI Corner: Cross-Border Investments and KAGAZ & KABZA

Documentation Challenges and Solutions for NRIs: Managing Property Rights Across Borders

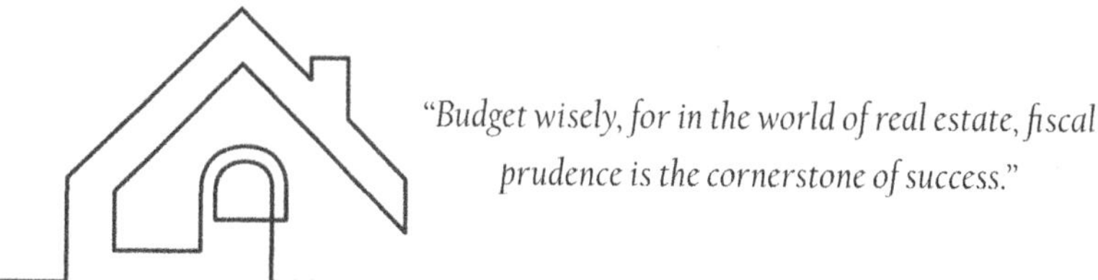

Introduction:

For Non-Resident Indians (NRIs), investing in Indian real estate can be both a sentiment-driven decision and a strategic wealth-building opportunity. However, navigating the complexities of cross-border investments and ensuring property rights can be challenging. This subchapter, titled 'NRI Corner: Cross-Border Investments and KAGAZ & KABZA', is dedicated to NRIs seeking to invest in the Indian real estate market. We will explore the unique documentation challenges they face and how KAGAZ (Knowledge of Necessary Documents) and KABZA (Safeguarding Your Property Rights) can be their trusted companions in this journey.

Documentation Challenges for NRIs:

Investing in Indian real estate as an NRI involves dealing with specific documentation challenges due to physical distances and jurisdictional variations.

Overseas Identity and Verification:

NRIs often face difficulties in establishing their identity and verifying documents from abroad. The process of notarising documents, obtaining an apostille or visiting the Indian embassy can be cumbersome.

Example: An NRI based in the USA had to notarise and apostille several property-related documents before initiating a transaction in India, which required extra time and effort. The journey to the Indian embassy, the authentication process and subsequent courier services added to the overall timeline and expenses.

Power of Attorney:

NRIs frequently rely on power of attorney (PoA) to facilitate property transactions in India. Drafting, notarising and ensuring the legality of PoA documents is critical. Traditionally, NRIs would draft the PoA, have it notarised in the country of their residence and then have it attested by the Indian consulate or embassy. The attested PoA would then need to be stamped and registered in India to be legally valid.

Fact: In 2022, the Indian government introduced e-PoA services, allowing NRIs to execute PoA documents online, simplifying the process. These digital services aim to make the PoA process more efficient, reducing the time and effort required for NRIs to manage their property transactions in India.

However, some NRIs may still face challenges in adopting these digital solutions due to a lack of awareness or hesitation in transitioning from traditional practices.

Taxation and Compliance:

Navigating Indian tax laws and compliance requirements from abroad can be complex for NRIs. Understanding tax implications, including capital gains tax and TDS (Tax Deducted at Source), is crucial.

Case Study: An NRI in the UAE sought professional advice to navigate the complexities of the Indian tax system, ensuring compliance and minimising tax liability. The process involved consultations with tax experts in both countries, which required extra effort and coordination.

Property Rights and Inheritance:

Ensuring that property rights and inheritance matters are legally sound is a significant concern for NRIs. They must be aware of the relevant property laws and inheritance regulations in India.

Example: An NRI residing in Canada consulted legal experts to draft a will specifying the distribution of his Indian properties among his heirs, ensuring clarity and compliance with Indian inheritance laws. This involved extensive discussions with legal professionals in both countries, adding complexity to the process.

KAGAZ & KABZA Solutions for NRIs:

KAGAZ and KABZA principles can significantly benefit NRIs investing in Indian real estate by addressing these documentation challenges.

Digital Documentation and Verification:

KAGAZ promotes the digitisation of documents, making it easier for NRIs to access and verify their paperwork online. Secure digital platforms and e-signature services simplify the document verification process.

Fact: In 2021, the government launched the 'DigiLocker' platform, enabling NRIs to access and store their important documents digitally. While this initiative has simplified access to documents, NRIs may still encounter challenges in convincing traditional institutions to accept digital copies for property transactions.

Streamlined Power of Attorney:

KABZA emphasises the importance of clear and legally sound PoA documents. NRIs can use the simplified e-PoA services to create and manage PoA documents without the need for physical presence.

Example: An NRI in Australia utilised e-PoA services to grant a family member in India the authority to manage and transact on his behalf, ensuring a seamless process. This transition to digital PoA services required understanding the new platform and educating the involved parties on its benefits.

Tax Planning and Compliance Guidance:

KAGAZ offers insights into taxation and compliance. NRIs can seek advice from financial experts who specialise in NRI tax matters to ensure they are fully informed about their tax liabilities and deductions.

Case Study: An NRI in the UK consulted an Indian tax expert to optimise his tax planning, resulting in reduced tax liability and enhanced returns on his Indian real estate investments. However, this process involved multiple consultations and coordination between tax experts in different countries.

Property Rights Protection:

KABZA principles extend to protecting property rights, including those of NRIs. NRIs can benefit from legal expertise to understand and navigate property laws and inheritance regulations in India.

Fact: In 2023, the Indian government introduced simplified property inheritance procedures for NRIs, streamlining the transfer of property rights to heirs. This initiative has reduced legal complexities, but NRIs may still need guidance to ensure a smooth inheritance process.

Cross-Border Estate Planning:

NRIs can explore cross-border estate planning to ensure that their Indian real estate investments align with their overall estate goals.

Example: An NRI family based in Singapore engaged estate planning experts to create a comprehensive strategy that considered their Indian properties, ensuring a smooth transition to their heirs. This involved coordinating with professionals in multiple countries to develop a cohesive estate plan.

NRI Guidelines for Home Buying and Tax Considerations:

Investing in Indian real estate as an NRI can be a rewarding venture, but it comes with specific tax implications. Here's an overview of key tax considerations and guidelines for NRIs looking to invest in Indian properties:

NRI Tax Laws and Residential Status:

Residential Status: Determine your residential status in India based on your physical presence during the financial year. Understanding your status as an NRI or RNOR is crucial for tax purposes.

1. **NRI (Non-Resident Indian):** An individual is considered an NRI if their total stay in India during a financial year (April 1 to March 31) is less than 182 days.

2. **RNOR (Resident but Not Ordinary Resident):** An individual qualifies as an RNOR if they meet specific conditions regarding their stay in India over the preceding years.

Taxable Income: NRIs are taxed only on income earned or accrued in India. Income generated abroad is generally not taxable in India.

Tax Rates: NRIs are subject to income tax rates similar to resident Indians on their Indian income. Special rates apply to certain types of income like long-term capital gains.

TDS (Tax Deducted at Source):

TDS Application: TDS is applicable to various payments made to NRIs, including rent, interest, dividends and capital gains.

TDS Reduction Strategies:

1. **Apply for Lower TDS Certificate (Form 13):** NRIs can apply for a Lower Tax Deduction Certificate under Section 197 of the Income Tax Act to reduce TDS on property sales.

2. **Furnish Necessary Documents:** Provide sale agreements, PAN, details of the buyer and seller, valuation reports and other relevant documents.

3. **Tax Planning and Consultation:** Seek advice from tax consultants specialising in NRI taxation to structure the sale transaction and minimise the tax burden.

Repatriation of Funds:

Repatriation Limits: NRIs can repatriate funds from India to foreign accounts within specific limits and after fulfilling necessary requirements.

Compliance with RBI Regulations: Repatriation of funds from property sales requires compliance with RBI regulations, including furnishing Form 15CA and 15CB.

Exemptions and Deductions:

Tax Deductions: NRIs can avail deductions and exemptions similar to resident Indians under different sections of the Income Tax Act, such as Sections 80C and 24(b).

Property Sale and TDS:

Section 195 and TDS: Section 195 requires TDS deduction by the buyer before paying the sale proceeds to the NRI seller.

TDS Rates: TDS rates for property sale range from 20% for long-term capital gains to 30% for short-term gains.

TDS Reduction for Improved Cash Flows: Applying for a TDS certificate (Form 13) to reduce the TDS liability on property sale.

Section 197 for Lower TDS: Obtaining a Lower Deduction Certificate under Section 197 to lessen TDS on property sale.

TDS Refund and Claims:

TDS Refunds: NRIs can claim TDS refunds on various income sources, including property transactions.

Section 195 Compliance: TDS deductions under Section 195 apply to most payments made to NRIs, ensuring tax compliance.

Process for Selling Property as an NRI:

Selling property in India involves several steps and compliance requirements. Here's a step-by-step guide for NRIs:

1. **Eligibility to Sell:** Ensure the property is legally acquired and ascertain the type of property (residential, commercial, agricultural) you own, as certain restrictions apply to agricultural land, plantation property and farmhouses.

2. **Documentation Check:** Ensure all property documents are in order, including the sale deed, title deed, possession letter, property tax receipts and other relevant paperwork.

3. **Tax Implications:** Understand the tax implications of selling property, including capital gains tax (20% for long-term and 30% for short-term gains) and TDS deductions.

4. **TDS Deduction:** The buyer must deduct TDS at the time of payment. The rate varies based on the type of gain (short-term or long-term) and the applicable DTAA benefits.

5. **Tax Clearance Certificate:** Obtain a Tax Clearance Certificate from the Income Tax Department post-sale, ensuring all applicable taxes are paid.

6. **Repatriation of Funds:** Comply with RBI regulations for repatriating sale proceeds. Submit Form 15CA and 15CB and ensure the funds are credited to your NRE or NRO account as per repatriation limits.

7. **Power of Attorney:** If you cannot be physically present, assign a PoA to a trusted person in India to complete the sale on your behalf.

8. **Capital Gains Account Scheme (CGAS):** If you cannot immediately reinvest the capital gains, deposit the funds in a CGAS account to defer tax liability until reinvestment.

9. **Consult Legal and Tax Advisors:** Engage with legal and tax experts specialising in NRI property transactions to ensure compliance with all legal and tax obligations.

Investing in Indian real estate from overseas as an NRI is a rewarding endeavour that requires careful planning and diligent documentation. KAGAZ & KABZA principles offer solutions to the unique challenges faced by NRIs. By leveraging digital documentation, streamlined PoA services, expert tax guidance and property rights protection, NRIs can make informed investments, secure their property rights and navigate the complexities of cross-border real estate transactions.

Understanding NRI tax laws and guidelines is crucial for making informed real estate investments in India. Applying for TDS reduction certificates and knowing how to claim TDS refunds can optimise your investment experience. By familiarising yourself with these regulations, you can navigate the complexities of property transactions confidently and make the most of your investment journey in India.

As we continue our journey through the Indian real estate landscape, the next subchapter will delve into the intricacies of legal and taxation matters in real estate. It will explore how KAGAZ and KABZA can guide individuals through the complexities of Indian real estate law and taxation, providing a strong foundation for success.

5.7. The Comprehensive Legal and Tax Handbook

KAGAZ in Real Estate Taxation: KABZA's Role in Legal Frameworks

"Accuracy in documentation ensures that your property story is written without loopholes."

Introduction:

In the complex landscape of Indian real estate, understanding the legal and tax aspects is not just prudent; it's essential. This subchapter, titled 'The Comprehensive Legal and Tax Handbook', serves as your guide to the intricate world of real estate taxation and legal frameworks. We will explore how KAGAZ (Knowledge of Necessary Documents) plays a pivotal role in real estate taxation, while KABZA (Safeguarding Your Property Rights) ensures compliance within legal frameworks. By mastering these aspects, you'll be equipped to navigate the challenging terrain of legalities and taxes in the Indian real estate sector.

KAGAZ in Real Estate Taxation:

Real estate taxation in India is a multifaceted domain and KAGAZ principles can significantly impact your understanding and management of these taxes.

Property Ownership Records and Tax Assessment:

KAGAZ emphasises the importance of maintaining accurate property ownership records. These records are the foundation for property tax assessments, which can vary based on factors like property type, location and usage.

Example 1: Rahul owns multiple properties in a city, including a residential apartment and a commercial office space. Each property falls under different tax jurisdictions, subjecting him to varying tax rates. Rahul's meticulous property records, including sale deeds, occupancy certificates and property layouts, enable him to accurately classify each property, ensuring he pays the correct property tax rate for each.

Example 2: Meera inherited a piece of agricultural land from her family in a rural area. She decided to convert the land into a residential property and build a farmhouse. However, without proper documentation of the land conversion and land use change, she encountered challenges during the property tax assessment. KAGAZ's principles emphasise the importance of documenting such changes, helping individuals like Meera avoid unnecessary tax complications.

Transaction History and Capital Gains Tax:

KAGAZ promotes thorough documentation of transaction history. When it comes to selling property, capital gains tax is a critical consideration. Long-term and short-term capital gains are taxed differently and documentation plays a pivotal role in determining the applicable tax rate.

Example 1: Rajesh, a property investor, sold an apartment he had owned for six years. Since he held the property for more than two years, it qualified as a long-term capital asset, subject to a lower capital gains tax rate. His ability to provide well-documented records of the property's purchase, improvements and sale was instrumental in availing this tax benefit, resulting in substantial tax savings.

Example 2: Preeti, who recently inherited a property from her parents and sold it within a year, was subject to short-term capital gains tax. KAGAZ's principles had not been followed in maintaining the transaction history and property records. As a result, Preeti faced a higher tax rate and a larger tax liability on the sale proceeds.

Stamp Duty and GST Compliance:

Stamp duty and Goods and Services Tax (GST) are integral parts of property transactions. KAGAZ ensures that property buyers and sellers have accurate documentation to calculate and comply with these taxes.

Example 1: Avinash and Neha decided to purchase a newly constructed apartment in Pune. They meticulously verified the builder's credentials, including GST registration and compliance, before finalising the deal. This proactive approach ensured that they didn't face any unexpected tax liabilities or disputes during the transaction.

Example 2: Sameer, a first-time property buyer, rushed into a property purchase without thoroughly examining the GST implications. After the purchase, he discovered that the builder had not passed on the GST benefits, resulting in a higher cost. This situation could have been avoided with proper documentation and GST compliance checks.

Property Valuation and Wealth Tax:

KAGAZ principles encourage property owners to maintain proper documentation related to property valuation. While wealth tax has been abolished, property valuation remains relevant for calculating other taxes and for asset management.

Example 1: Anita, a property owner in Delhi, decided to rent out her commercial space. Proper documentation of the property's fair market value helped her determine the rental income and deductions available to her. This not only streamlined her tax filing process but also maximised her returns from the property.

Example 2: Avinash, who owned multiple properties in Mumbai, engaged a property valuation expert to assess the current market value of his assets. This valuation played a crucial role in estate planning, ensuring a smooth transition of assets to his heirs while minimising inheritance tax implications.

KABZA's Role in Legal Frameworks:

KABZA complements KAGAZ by ensuring that your real estate transactions and holdings align with legal frameworks.

RERA Compliance:

The Real Estate (Regulation and Development) Act, commonly known as RERA, is a game-changer in Indian real estate. KABZA ensures that developers and builders adhere to RERA regulations, providing transparency and protection to homebuyers.

Example 1: Mega Builders, a real estate development company in Bangalore, faced legal repercussions due to non-compliance with RERA regulations. KABZA's role in legal frameworks emphasises the importance of complying with RERA's guidelines, including project registration, disclosure of project details and timely project completion. By aligning with these regulations, developers like Mega Builders can avoid legal complications and build trust among buyers.

Example 2: Rajiv, a homebuyer in Gurgaon, had his reservations about investing in an under-construction project due to past experiences of project delays and quality issues. However, his research revealed that the developer of the project had a strong track record of adhering to RERA guidelines, providing buyers with peace of mind and confidence in the investment.

Property Title Verification:

KABZA emphasises the importance of verifying property titles to avoid legal disputes. This involves ensuring that the property's title is free from encumbrances and disputes, providing peace of mind to buyers and investors.

Example 1: Sonia, a first-time homebuyer in Chennai, engaged a legal professional to conduct a thorough title search before finalising her property purchase. The title search revealed an ongoing dispute related to the property's ownership, prompting Sonia to reconsider the transaction. This diligence helped her avoid a potential legal quagmire.

Example 2: Arjun, another homebuyer in the same city, neglected to verify the property's title adequately. After completing the purchase, he discovered that the property had unresolved title issues dating back several years. Arjun's lack of due diligence resulted in a protracted legal battle and financial loss.

Environmental and Zoning Compliance:

Real estate developments must adhere to environmental and zoning regulations. KABZA ensures that developers comply with these laws, contributing to sustainable development and environmental protection.

Example 1: A real estate developer in Pune recognised the significance of adhering to environmental regulations while planning a new residential project. By implementing sustainable construction practices and obtaining necessary environmental clearances, the developer not only ensured compliance with legal frameworks but also attracted environmentally conscious buyers, enhancing the project's marketability.

Example 2: A developer in Hyderabad faced legal challenges due to violations of environmental regulations during the construction of a commercial complex. This oversight resulted in legal penalties and project delays, highlighting the importance of KABZA's role in ensuring environmental and zoning compliance.

Documentation for Legal Proceedings:

In the event of legal disputes, KABZA ensures that property owners have the necessary documentation to support their cases. This includes property records, agreements and communication records.

Example 1: Amit, a property owner in Mumbai, found himself in a legal dispute with a tenant over unpaid rent and property damage. Fortunately, Amit had meticulously maintained records of the lease agreement, rent receipts and communication with the tenant. This documentation played a pivotal role in resolving the dispute in his favour through a swift legal process.

Example 2: Nisha, a property seller, faced a legal challenge when a buyer claimed that she had not disclosed certain property defects during the transaction. Nisha's comprehensive documentation, including property inspection reports and communication logs, helped her establish transparency and fulfil her legal obligations.

In the intricate world of Indian real estate, mastering the legal and tax aspects is non-negotiable. This expanded subchapter has delved into the role of KAGAZ in real estate taxation and KABZA's significance in legal frameworks. By understanding and applying these principles, you not only ensure compliance with tax regulations but also protect your investments from legal pitfalls.

As we continue our exploration of the Indian real estate landscape, the next subchapter will serve as a guide for sustainable real estate practices. We will delve into 'Green Real Estate: Sustainability through KAGAZ & KABZA', focusing on eco-compliance and sustainable development in the context of Indian real estate.

5.8. Green Real Estate: Sustainability through KAGAZ & KABZA

Eco-Compliance and Documentation: Sustainable Development and Property Rights

"Property aspirations, like dreams, are the foundation upon which reality is built."

Introduction:

In the era of environmental consciousness, the real estate industry is undergoing a transformation toward sustainable practices. This subchapter, titled 'Green Real Estate: Sustainability through KAGAZ & KABZA', explores the crucial role that documentation and property rights play in promoting eco-compliance and sustainable development. We will delve into how KAGAZ (Knowledge of Necessary Documents) and KABZA (Safeguarding Your Property Rights) serve as guiding principles in the path toward green real estate. By integrating these principles, you'll not only contribute to a sustainable future but also safeguard your investments in the Indian real estate market.

Eco-Compliance and Documentation:

Eco-compliance in real estate involves adhering to environmental regulations, reducing carbon footprints and adopting eco-friendly construction practices. Proper documentation is a fundamental aspect of ensuring eco-compliance.

Environmental Clearances and Permits:

KAGAZ emphasises the importance of obtaining and maintaining records of environmental clearances and permits when undertaking real estate projects. These documents demonstrate compliance with environmental laws and regulations.

Example 1: A real estate developer in Mumbai embarked on a project that involved the construction of a residential complex near a protected wetland. To ensure eco-compliance, the developer secured the necessary environmental clearances and permits, allowing for responsible construction that protected the wetland's ecosystem. The documentation of these clearances played a crucial role in gaining community support and avoiding legal challenges.

Example 2: In contrast, a developer in Chennai proceeded with a construction project without obtaining the required environmental permits. This oversight led to legal actions, delays and financial penalties, highlighting the significance of KAGAZ's eco-compliance principles.

Sustainable Building Certifications:

Incorporating sustainable building certifications like LEED (Leadership in Energy and Environmental Design) or GRIHA (Green Rating for Integrated Habitat Assessment) is a hallmark of green real estate. KAGAZ encourages developers and builders to maintain documentation of the certification process.

Example 1: A commercial real estate developer in Bangalore pursued LEED certification for their office building. Documentation of sustainable design features, energy-efficient systems and green construction materials played a pivotal role in achieving LEED Platinum certification. This not only attracted environmentally conscious tenants but also resulted in long-term cost savings on energy and maintenance.

Example 2: Another developer in Hyderabad ignored the importance of documenting sustainable practices during construction. Despite incorporating eco-friendly elements, they failed to pursue any certification. As a result, they missed out on the marketing advantages and potential cost savings associated with sustainable building certifications.

Waste Management and Recycling Documentation:

Proper disposal of construction and demolition waste is a key aspect of green real estate. KAGAZ highlights the importance of maintaining records related to waste management and recycling efforts.

Example 1: A residential builder in Pune implemented a comprehensive waste management and recycling program during the construction of a housing project. Detailed documentation of waste sorting, recycling processes and waste diversion rates not only ensured compliance with waste management regulations but also positioned the project as an environmentally responsible development.

Example 2: A different developer in the same city neglected to document waste management efforts, resulting in haphazard waste disposal practices. This not only led to environmental violations but also tarnished the project's reputation, affecting sales and investor confidence.

Sustainable Development and Property Rights:

Sustainable development goes beyond eco-compliance; it also involves responsible land use, conservation of natural resources and equitable property rights.

Land Use Planning and Conservation Easements:

KABZA plays a vital role in ensuring that land use planning aligns with sustainable development goals. Conservation easements, which limit the use of land for specific purposes like agriculture or wildlife conservation, are documented to protect natural resources.

Example 1: A landowner in Kerala, inspired by sustainable development principles, placed a conservation easement on a portion of their property to preserve a pristine forest area. This documentation ensured that the land could not be used for commercial purposes, contributing to local biodiversity conservation.

Example 2: In contrast, another landowner in the same state did not document the conservation easement on their property. When they later attempted to clear the land for development, they faced legal challenges from environmental groups and authorities, resulting in substantial fines and project delays.

Water Rights and Sustainable Usage:

Sustainable development also involves responsible water usage and documentation of water rights. KABZA ensures that property owners are aware of their rights and responsibilities regarding water sources.

Example 1: A farmer in Rajasthan who owned agricultural land documented their water rights and committed to sustainable water usage practices. This not only ensured the efficient use of water resources but also positioned the property as an eco-friendly investment.

Example 2: Conversely, a landowner in the same region did not document water rights and engaged in unsustainable water extraction. This led to conflicts with neighbouring landowners, legal battles and fines for violating water usage regulations.

Community Land Trusts and Sustainable Communities:

KABZA supports the concept of community land trusts, which enable communities to collectively own and manage land for sustainable development. Documentation of community land trust agreements is crucial to safeguard property rights and ensure sustainable community development.

Example 1: A group of residents in Himachal Pradesh established a community land trust to protect a pristine forested area from commercial development. By documenting their trust agreement and sustainable land use practices, they preserved the forest as a shared community asset, promoting biodiversity and eco-conscious living.

Example 2: In a different region, a lack of proper documentation and governance within a community land trust led to disputes over land use and resource management. This resulted in division within the community and hindered efforts for sustainable development.

Tax Incentives for Green Real Estate:

KAGAZ also extends its reach into understanding tax incentives and benefits available for green real estate projects. Documentation of these incentives is essential for maximising financial advantages.

Example 1: A developer in Bengaluru undertook a green residential project that incorporated energy-efficient features and sustainable materials. By documenting the project's adherence to green building standards, the developer became eligible for tax incentives, resulting in significant cost savings.

Example 2: In contrast, a developer in Delhi initiated a similar green project but failed to maintain proper documentation of the eco-friendly elements. As a consequence, they missed out on tax incentives, impacting the project's overall financial viability.

In the dynamic landscape of Indian real estate, sustainability is not just a buzzword; it's a necessity. This expanded subchapter has explored the role of KAGAZ in eco-compliance and KABZA's significance in sustainable development and property rights. By integrating these principles, you not only contribute to a greener future but also secure your investments in the Indian real estate market.

As we conclude our journey through the diverse facets of Indian real estate, we hope this comprehensive guide has equipped you with the knowledge and insights needed to navigate this complex landscape with confidence and success.

"A home is more than just walls and a roof; it's the heart of your family's story."

"In the ever-changing world of real estate, those who succeed are those who plan and adapt. By combining strategic foresight with calculated action, we turn knowledge into prosperity and investments into legacies."

Checklists for 'Kagaz & Kabza' as a Gift from Author Sanjjay Jain

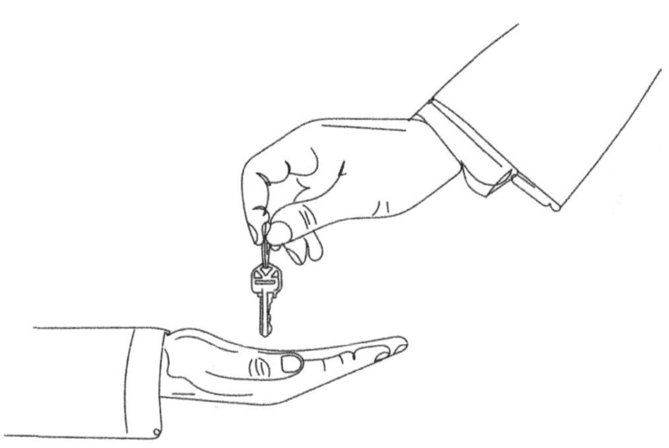

Unlock Your Exclusive Reader Benefits

Thank you for joining me on this enlightening journey through "Kagaz & Kabza." To further enhance your understanding and application of the insights shared in this book, I've prepared an exclusive set of resources just for you!

Inside, you'll find detailed checklists that can help you navigate the complex terrain of property documentation and ownership—a perfect companion to the strategies and stories we've explored together.

How to Access Your Gift:

1. Locate the QR code found on the next page.

2. Use your smartphone camera or a QR code scanner app to scan the code.

3. You'll be directed to a special landing page on my website.

Once there, simply follow the instructions to download your exclusive content. This additional material is designed to empower you with practical tools and deepen your understanding, ensuring you're well-equipped to tackle the challenges discussed in the book.

Enjoy your reading and the resources waiting for you—your journey to mastering the kagaz and kabza doesn't end here!

First-Time Buyer Checklist:

1. **Real Estate Terminology Checklist**: Understand basic terms such as equity, home loan, Loan Against Property (LAP) etc.

2. **First-Time Buyer's Financing Checklist**: Detailed steps for securing a mortgage, comparing loan types, understanding interest rates and calculating down payments.

3. **Essential Features in a First Home Checklist**: Factors like size, location, neighbourhood safety, nearby amenities and resale value considerations.

4. **Home Buying Step-by-Step Checklist**: From attending open houses to negotiating with sellers, arranging home inspections and closing the deal.

5. **Legal Documentation Specific to India Checklist**: Checklist for essential legal documents like Sale Deed, Title Deed, Encumbrance Certificate, Khata Certificate, etc.

6. **RERA Compliance Checklist**: Ensure compliance with the Real Estate (Regulation and Development) Act, including project registration, disclosure of project details, etc.

7. **Property Registration Process Checklist:** Step-by-step guide to property registration in India, including documentation, NOC, Completion Certificate from concerned authorities, fees and timelines.

8. **Dispute Resolution Mechanisms Checklist:** Understand available options for resolving real estate disputes in India, such as consumer forums, arbitration and litigation.

Regular Buyer Checklist:

1. **Property Evaluation Techniques Checklist:** Advanced methods for assessing property condition, historical value appreciation and potential future growth.

2. **Effective Property Management Checklist:** Regular maintenance schedules, tenant management for rental properties and handling property-related disputes.

3. **Renovation ROI Calculation Checklist:** Estimate the return on investment for various types of renovations and upgrades.

4. **Second Home Purchase Considerations Checklist:** Specific considerations for vacation homes or investment properties, including location-specific risks.

Investor Checklist:

1. **Market Trend Analysis Checklist:** Tools and indicators to analyse real estate market trends and predict profitable investment opportunities.

2. **Diversification Strategies in Real Estate Checklist:** Spread investments across residential, commercial and land to mitigate risks.

3. **Property Flip Checklist:** Steps for buying, renovating and selling properties for profit, including timeline planning and budget management.

4. **Commercial Property Investment Checklist**: Special considerations for purchasing office spaces, retail locations or industrial properties.

5. **NRI Investment Checklist**: Guide for Non-Resident Indians (NRIs) looking to invest in Indian real estate, covering legal considerations, taxation rules and managing property from abroad.

Comprehensive Due Diligence:

1. **Title Search and Insurance Checklist**: Detailed steps for conducting a title search and securing title insurance.

2. **Property Legal Check Checklist**: Ensure no legal encumbrances or pending litigations that could affect the purchase.

3. **Local Regulations and Permissions Checklist**: Checklist for local building permissions, environmental clearances and other regulatory approvals.

Financial Management and Tax Planning:

1. **Property Investment Tax Implications Checklist**: Detailed guide on property tax, capital gains tax and possible tax exemptions.

2. **Mortgage Refinancing Checklist**: Consider refinancing to take advantage of lower interest rates or improved credit scores.

3. **Estate Planning and Real Estate Checklist**: Incorporate real estate into estate planning, including trusts and inheritances.

Sustainable and Green Investment:

1. **Green Certification Processes Checklist**: Steps to obtain LEED or other green building certifications.

2. **Cost-Benefit Analysis of Eco-Friendly Upgrades Checklist**: Evaluate the financial and environmental benefits of sustainable upgrades.

Bibliography

This curated list of references is designed to offer readers a wide-ranging overview of the real estate sector, covering foundational theories, practical investment strategies and the latest trends, with a special emphasis on the dynamics of the Indian real estate market. Whether you're a student, professional or enthusiast, these resources will deepen your understanding and enhance your knowledge base.

1. Anderson, J., & Wang, K. (2016). Real Estate Economics. Routledge.

2. Kiyosaki, R. T. (1997). Rich Dad Poor Dad: What the Rich Teach Their Kids About Money That the Poor and Middle Class Do Not! Warner Books.

3. Barris, J. D., & Weinstein, J. M. (2018). Urban Economics and Real Estate: Theory and Policy. John Wiley & Sons.

4. Geltner, D. M., Miller, N. G., Clayton, J., & Eichholtz, P. (2019). Commercial Real Estate Analysis and Investments. Cengage Learning.

5. Ling, D. C., & Archer, W. R. (2017). Real Estate Principles: A Value Approach. McGraw-Hill Education.

6. Poorvu, W. J., & Cruickshank, J. L. (2017). The Real Estate Game: The Intelligent Guide to Decision-Making and Investment. Simon and Schuster.

7. Saglam, M. (2019). Real Estate Finance: Theory and Practice. Springer.

8. Turnball, G. K., & Miles, M. E. (2018). Residential Real Estate Finance. Routledge.

9. White, R. S., & Sirmans, G. S. (2018). The Real Estate Challenge: Capitalising on Change. Routledge.

10. Shaw, A. (2019). Real Estate and Urban Development in South Asia. Routledge.

11. Mathur, O. P., & Thakur, R. P. (2020). Financing Urban Infrastructure in India: Challenges and Solutions. Sage Publications.

12. Datta, A. (2021). The Illegal City: Space, Law and Gender in a Delhi Squatter Settlement. Ashgate.

13. Bhan, G., Srinivas, S., & Watson, V. (Eds.). (2018). The Routledge Companion to Planning in the Global South. Routledge.

14. Indian Government (2016). Real Estate (Regulation and Development) Act, 2016. Ministry of Housing and Urban Affairs.

15. Institute for Housing and Urban Development Studies (IHS) (2018). Affordable Housing Policies and Practices in Indian Cities. IHS.

16. National Association of Realtors India (NAR) (2020). Indian Real Estate: Market Trends and Opportunities. NAR India.

17. Confederation of Real Estate Developers' Associations of India (CREDAI) (2020). Indian Real Estate: Trends and Insights. CREDAI.

18. National Real Estate Development Council (NAREDCO) (2021). Indian Real Estate Outlook: Opportunities and Challenges. NAREDCO.

19. Knight Frank (2021). Global Residential Cities Index Q2 2021. Knight Frank Research.

20. Reserve Bank of India (2022). Master Direction on KYC Norms/Anti-Money Laundering Measures/Combating of Financing of Terrorism. RBI/2021-22/100.

21. Kumar, N. A. (2021). Real Estate Regulation and Development Act, 2016: A Conceptual Analysis. International Journal of Legal Science and Innovation, 3(1), 1-12.

22. National Housing Bank (2022). Housing Price Index (HPI) Q3 2021-22. National Housing Bank.

23. Reserve Bank of India (2021). Handbook of Statistics on the Indian Economy. Reserve Bank of India.

24. Yadav, A., & Sharma, R. (2018). Indian Real Estate—A Scenario Analysis. Real Estate Finance, 35(4), 9-16.

IndiePress

The best route your story can take.

To publish your own book, contact us.

We publish poetry collections, short story collections, novellas and novels.

contact@http://indiepress.in/

Instagram- indie_press

Made in the USA
Monee, IL
07 July 2026